"Sunday school curriculum is relentlessly moralistic. That is, it tells you *what* to do, but not *how* to do it. Jack Klumpenhower shows us *how* by taking us back to the person and work of Christ. Every Sunday school teacher should read this book."

    Paul Miller, Director of seeJesus; author of *A Praying Life* and *A Loving Life*

"Klumpenhower states the problem well: 'Today, a frightening number of kids are growing up in churches and Christian homes without ever being captured by the gospel of Jesus.' We want them to know about Jesus, but we leave them with lessons about behavior and they leave the church as soon as possible. Here's a book that sweetly, masterfully, and powerfully tells us what the gospel really is and how it can really change a child's life and eternity."

    Bryan Chapell, Author of *Christ-Centered Preaching*; pastor, Grace Presbyterian Church in Peoria, IL

"*Show Them Jesus* is a must read for every youth worker, children's ministry teacher, parent, and VBS volunteer. Jack Klumpenhower does a masterful job helping us learn how to discover the gospel connections in every Bible story. In sharing example after example from his years of experience, Jack gives the reader a front-row seat in his classroom to learn how to give children a 'rock-their-world' vision of Jesus. This is the perfect training tool for pastors and children's ministry leaders to use to train their teachers. I'll be buying a copy for all my children's ministry leaders."

    Marty Machowski, Family Life Pastor, Covenant Fellowship Church in Glen Mills, PA; author of the *Gospel Story for Kids* curriculum

"Jack's book has done a very rare thing—he has taken the message of grace and applied it simply and directly to both teachers' hearts and the children they shepherd. He doesn't settle for mere external obedience in his students but bravely and compassionately goes much deeper, seeking out their hearts. This is a great application of Serge's values to a central part of every church—its children."

    Bob Osborne, Executive Director, Serge

"*Show Them Jesus* deals with the tough questions that keep children's ministry leaders up at night. How do I encourage kids to repent and obey without becoming a legalist? Should I tone down Old Testament violence when I'm teaching fourth graders? Klumpenhower answers these questions and more with his eyes on Jesus from first to last. But he doesn't just speak to the head. He engages heart and hands as well, giving teachers an inspiring and practical framework for preparing Bible lessons, classroom environments, and family ministry where Jesus is the focus. I plan to purchase a copy for every volunteer in our children's ministry."

Jared Kennedy, Family Pastor, Sojourn Community Church in Louisville, KY

"The most common way of teaching a Bible story to children involves holding up the main human character and encouraging (or discouraging) children to be like him or her. *Show Them Jesus: Teaching the Gospel to Kids* provides welcome relief. The book is packed full of biblical reasons, practical guidance, and bountiful examples for teachers and parents who want to show children Jesus when they teach the Bible."

Starr Meade, Author of *Training Hearts, Teaching Minds: Family Devotions based on the Shorter Catechism* and *Mighty Acts of God: a Family Bible Story Book*

"In *Show Them Jesus*, Jack Klumpenhower tells how to make Spirit-fed renewal, which springs from a foundation of love for Jesus, the overarching theme of our teaching. He impresses on us the importance of being 'good-news' teachers who 'exit' every Bible story through the cross of Christ. Make your aim in teaching to build in your kids love for Jesus, because that's where the Christian life begins. Read this book for your kids; and reread it for yourself."

Nancy Winter, Curriculum writer and editor; long-time Sunday school teacher.

"This book is a must read for every Christian and challenges us to ask the question: How are we handling the good news about Jesus? Do we really believe that Jesus is the goal of God's great story of redemption—'the way, the truth, and the life'? Jack reminds us that our teaching and application of the Scripture is to be unflinchingly centered on Jesus. Why? So we can all fall more in love with Him and worship Him wholeheartedly!"

Rosemarie Green, Director of Children's Ministry, New Life Church, Glenside, PA

SHOW THEM JESUS

Teaching the Gospel to Kids

Jack Klumpenhower

New
Growth
Press

newgrowthpress.com

New Growth Press, Greensboro, NC 27401
Copyright © 2014 by Jack Klumpenhower.

Unless otherwise indicated, Scripture quotations are taken from *The Holy Bible, English Standard Version*.˚ Copyright © 2000; 2001 by Crossway Bibles, a division of Good News Publishers. Used by permission. All rights reserved.

Scripture quotations marked (NIrV) are taken from the Holy Bible, NEW INTERNATIONAL READER'S VERSION®. Copyright © 1996, 1998 Biblica. All rights reserved throughout the world. Used by permission of Biblica.

Scripture quotations marked (NIV 1984) are taken from the *Holy Bible*, New International Version®, NIV®. Copyright © 1973, 1978, 1984 by International Bible Society. Used by permission of Zondervan. All rights reserved.

Cover Design: Faceout Studio, faceoutbooks.com
Interior Typesetting: Lisa Parnell, lparnell.com

ISBN 978-1-939946-39-3 (Print)
ISBN 978-1-939946-40-9 (eBook)

Library of Congress Cataloging-in-Publication Data
Klumpenhower, Jack, 1963–
  Show them Jesus : teaching the gospel to kids / Jack Klumpenhower.
    pages cm
  Includes bibliographical references and index.
  ISBN 978-1-939946-39-3
  1. Church work with children. 2. Christian education of children. 3. Jesus Christ. I. Title.
  BV639.C4K58 2014
  268'.432—dc23
                                                                    2013037869

Printed in India

28 27 26 25 24 23 22 21   10 11 12 13 14

Contents

Acknowledgements

This book never would have happened without the support of my wife, Jodie, who encouraged me to keep writing even when I wondered if I was wasting my time. The team at New Growth Press and the staff at Serge, especially Bob Osborne, also kept this project moving when I got bogged down. I owe them all much thanks for their faith in me and their kind help.

I would be terribly remiss if I did not also acknowledge the men who through the years have served as my pastors—especially Clyde Godwin, Rick Downs, Hunter Dockery, Jeff Dobesh, and my dad, Gary Klumpenhower. Their gospel preaching has fed my soul week after week and trained my mind to focus on our Savior. Their faithfulness in showing *me* Jesus has seeped into every page of this book in ways I could never count.

Introduction
The Crew of Seventy-Two

The church I attended had a problem. It attracted many families, and parents eagerly brought their children to Sunday school and to midweek youth meetings—all good things. The trouble was, there never seemed to be enough volunteers to teach all those kids. Since I *did* teach, I was invited to help solve the problem.

We tried everything. Each year as the dreaded recruitment season arrived, the pastor issued appeals from the pulpit. We printed bulletin inserts. We personally asked our friends in the church to consider teaching. We begged for volunteers. But people kept telling us they were too busy, or that they weren't good at teaching.

So we made teaching easier. The church staff prepared all materials. An easy-to-follow lesson with games and crafts was waiting each week for the teacher, who simply had to show up. And although we held a weekly prayer meeting for teachers, we stressed that attending prayer was purely optional.

The teacher shortage just grew worse. You can probably see what we were doing wrong, but I didn't get it until one day when I was trying to talk another guy into becoming a teacher. I still remember the ridiculously insulting words I blurted out. I told him, "It's easy. Most of the work is done for you. And I think you'd be perfect for the job."

I might as well have used the old line that any idiot could do it, and that he was just the idiot I had in mind. My friend gave me an odd look, and I realized how foolish I'd been. I'd forgotten that although teachers do want support, no one likes to give even a minute of their time for ministry that's so easy it must be unimportant. And I'd arrogantly figured I was the sort of devoted teacher who might spend hours working on a lesson for the sake of Jesus, but others were not. It's a mistake I never want to make again.

So, then. There are many good books designed to make your teaching easier, but this is not one of them.

A Job with Jesus

Luke's Gospel tells how Jesus faced a problem similar to the teacher shortage. He was looking for workers to proclaim the kingdom of God. A series of prospects offered to help, on their terms. Jesus turned them down. He spoke of the work involved and the cost. Then he appointed seventy-two others to do the job. "The harvest is plentiful, but the laborers are few. Therefore pray earnestly to the Lord of the harvest to send out laborers into his harvest. Go your way; behold, I am sending you out as lambs in the midst of wolves. Carry no moneybag, no knapsack, no sandals, and greet no one on the road" (Luke 10:2–4).

Later, we learn what happened: "The seventy-two returned with joy, saying, 'Lord, even the demons are subject to us in your name!' And he said to them, 'I saw Satan fall like lightning from heaven. Behold, I have given you authority to tread on serpents and scorpions, and over all the power of the enemy, and nothing shall hurt you. Nevertheless, do not rejoice in this, that the spirits are subject to you, but rejoice that your names are written in heaven'" (Luke 10:17–20).

Jesus tells us that the work of proclaiming God's kingdom is dangerous. It takes courage. It demands earnest prayer. It's more about faith than giftedness, and it requires no resources other than those

God provides. It's a high-stakes spiritual battle, using supernatural weapons. Anyone who's willing to engage the fight on this level is needed for the cause. Such an adventurer will reap a rare mix of power, humility, and wide-eyed joy.

Doesn't that sound better than the namby-pamby Sunday school I was trying to sell?

As I've talked with other committed teachers—those at church as well as parents who teach about Jesus at home—I've finally learned that what Jesus was talking about is why they keep at it. They want to make a real difference, for God and for their kids. They know it's hard work; they know that the devil Jesus spoke of will fight back. That's okay. They feel called by God and are itching to speak the good news of Jesus in all its wonder—whatever that takes.

None of us does this well all the time. We get busy or tired or sloppy. We too often give in to mediocre expectations. But amid this slumber, we dream of being like the seventy-two. So we need to encourage each other to live up to our calling.

That's the purpose of this book.

WHY THOSE KIDS REALLY, REALLY NEED YOU

This book's main point is that we are called to teach the good news— all Jesus is and all he's done by his life, death, and resurrection to save those who're joined to him—and to treasure it as we work with kids. Since most prepackaged lessons and family devotionals don't do this, you'll need to make a deliberate effort. However, your effort will be doing the kids you teach a profound service.

Today, a frightening number of kids are growing up in churches and Christian homes without ever being captured by the gospel of Jesus. As children and teenagers they may seem to be believers, but then they reach their college and young-adult years and quit. They quit church—and any growing commitment to Jesus.

These kids actually have good reasons to quit. They look back and realize that they learned much about Christian behavior and churchy experiences, but whatever they learned about Jesus didn't really change them. They never saw him so strikingly that he became their one, overriding hope and their greatest love. They were never convinced that Jesus is better—a zillion times better—than anything and everything else.

Our goal must be for kids to catch this rock-their-world vision of Jesus. Is this far-fetched? Not at all. We have the message of God's love in Christ. We also have prayer and the Holy Spirit. We *have* the weapons to win this supernatural war. Knowing this, we must faithfully show kids, at every opportunity, how Jesus *is* that much better. We must also believe it ourselves, so that our lives among these kids confirm Jesus's power to change sinners.

Yes, in some ways it's hard. But because it's built on the good news—"your names are written in heaven"—rather than how "successful" we are, it isn't a burden. It's world-shaking, yet pressure-free.

How does this work? Let me share one example.

A SCARY LESSON

A few years ago I was teaching a large group of elementary kids from the book of Joshua. I taught how God brought his people through the Jordan River and toppled the walls of Jericho. From there, the curriculum I was using skipped a chapter—the story of Achan.

Achan was an Israelite soldier. He spurned a direct command from God by taking some of the plunder of Jericho for himself. His sin was uncovered when God caused the Israelites to be routed in a subsequent battle. To reveal whose sin was responsible, God used a dread-filled process of picking first the tribe, then the clan, then the family at fault. The members of the guilty family came forward one by one, and God picked Achan. So the people stoned Achan, along with his wife, children, and livestock. Then they set them on fire and heaped stones on their charred bodies. Only after that did God turn from his anger.

Well now, it's easy to see why that story gets skipped.

What should I do? I don't like picking through the Bible for just the cheery parts, but my group of kids was fairly young. I was worried that the lesson might be too scary. I finally decided I could teach about Achan—*if* I made sure that the good news of Jesus was my theme.

One of my helpers that day was also the mom of a student. Just before class she asked what the lesson was, and when I told her she became worried. Her daughter got nightmares, she explained. Tense stories often brought them on. I got a sick feeling. Surely I'd been stupid to think I could teach such a lesson to little kids. But there was no time to change it, so I taught about Achan. Dead soldiers. Selection process. Stoning. Fire. The whole ugly scene.

As I taught this, the concerned mom looked even more worried. So did some of the kids, who were particularly bothered that the other soldiers, family members, and animals got killed too. What had they done to deserve that? It was a good question, so I had the whole group gather around me as I sat on the floor with them.

"Yes, many were killed," I told them, "but that's what we should learn from this." I read to them the Bible's own commentary on the incident: "Didn't the LORD's anger come on the whole community of Israel? And Achan wasn't the only one who died because of his sin" (Joshua 22:20, NIrV).

"You see," I said, "just one man sinned, but many died. That's the lesson."

The kids gave me confused looks. It wasn't the sort of lesson anyone was expecting. I had their attention and pressed on.

"What if *you* sin? Or I sin? Does God punish us like he did Achan? Does anyone else get punished too? Or has God made a way to punish sin that has a better ending than this story has?"

The kids weren't sure. Several knew that God wouldn't be holy if he didn't punish sin. They also knew that God forgives. They weren't certain how it all fit together.

"The idea that a person might die for someone else's sin is very important," I said. "In our story, one man sinned but many died. But what if later in the Bible we found one man—just one man—who never sinned in his whole life, but still got punished? If that man never sinned but still died, then many could live."

They knew I was talking about Jesus.

I went on to tell how Jesus lived the sin-free life each of us don't. I told how out of all the tribes and clans and families of the world, only Jesus is not guilty—so God picked him. To die. To take our place. God selected Jesus to take the punishment we deserve so we don't have to stand sinful and quaking, waiting for judgment like Achan did.

"Your sin is very bad," I told the kids. "It can hurt many people. But God loves you so much that he sent his Son, Jesus, to become a man and die for your sin. Jesus was hurt most of all.

"I wasn't sure I should tell you this story because I thought it might be too scary. It's about the scariest thing ever—getting punished by God. But when you know the whole story, it isn't scary. If you belong to Jesus, he took your punishment and God becomes your Father. So I hope you won't be scared. You don't have to be scared of anything. Jesus makes the scariest thing of all go away."

I knew I'd done okay once it was over because the worried mom thanked me. She loved the story. The real surprise, though, came a few weeks later. The mom came up to me with a huge grin and told me her daughter's nightmares had stopped. The girl insisted it was because she knew that, due to Jesus, she didn't have to be scared anymore.

Well, that's the kind of result a teacher very rarely hears of, and my first reaction was skepticism. Could a little lesson about Jesus really cure such a problem? The nightmares would probably come back in time. But months went by and the mom remained delighted.

I finally came to see that *I* was the one who lacked faith in the power of the good news. In spite of teaching it, I never expected it to work so wonderfully. It was all due to Jesus, of course, who lived the story I had the privilege of repeating. There's no story like it. I should have expected such results.

When the account of Achan is taught at all, it's usually with the moral point that stealing is wrong. Okay, but that girl needed to hear the larger biblical point: that sin destroys life with God. Then she needed the biggest point of all—the theme of the whole Bible: that wherever sin destroys, Jesus heals.

That girl learned about Jesus and believed. She also discovered that belief in Jesus is life-changing, that he truly is better than anything else.

THE TEACHERS' MANIFESTO

So who am I to write this book? Well, I'm no expert. I've never been employed full-time by a school or church. I have stories to share, but they're as much about failure as success, and about what I've learned along the way. Some of it I'm not very good at yet. I still struggle.

I'm only a parent and volunteer who works with children and youth, leading lessons and other Christian activities. I'm just a Bible teacher—like you.

Yes, *you* are a teacher. Even if your role isn't teaching prepared lessons but one of the many other important jobs in children's or youth ministry, or if you lead your own kids in family devotions or home lessons—or want to start!—it's still teaching. Kids are watching and learning from you, and you have the job of showing them Jesus.

Most of what I'll share comes from my experience in the classroom because that's where I've learned to teach about Jesus. But once we grab hold of these ideas, they go wherever we go. I use them in more casual encounters with kids too, as well as at home with my own children. I'll help you apply them wherever *you* work with kids.

I'm going to assume that you too are a non-expert. The teachers Jesus recruited didn't start out well-equipped or particularly skilled either—so if you feel hesitant, or unsure you can teach a lesson like the one I just described, you're in a good place. I'm simply looking for parents, Sunday school teachers, youth workers, Bible club directors, camp counselors, song leaders—anyone who works with kids—to join me in this manifesto:

We pledge to teach the good news and show kids Jesus.

In this book, I'll suggest what that might look like. I'll tell my own story in the process, changing only names and other details to protect the kids. I'm going to let you see how I've done things because I know from experience that observing other teachers—for both faults and strengths—is the best way to improve. I'll also give examples of how I've taught many familiar Bible stories. None of my examples is the only good way to teach those stories, but all of them celebrate Jesus.

In the first half of the book, I'll explain *why* teaching the good news is so important and give you ways to get started. I hope this will renew your excitement to tell about Jesus. Nothing helps more than for you, the teacher, to develop an incurable case of "Jesus fever."

In the second half, I'll share what I've learned about *how* to show kids Jesus. After thirty-odd years of both my own teaching and picking up tips from others, I have ideas and methods that work. Please take what you can use, add to it, and fit it to your own ministry. Build on it. Make it better. Don't stop until your teaching is everything Jesus said it could be.

Whenever God's people rediscover the good news, revival often follows—so we will be playing with fire. Our manifesto is subversive. It will put us at odds with both devils and do-gooders. Keeping it will require an entire life of becoming more deeply dependent on the transforming work of God's Spirit. It's for those of us who want to raise our game to the level of the seventy-two.

Are you with me? Let's get started.

Section One
Why Teach the Good News?

Chapter 1

The One-Note Teacher

Because Jesus is everything we need

A sermon without Christ!
As well talk of a loaf of bread without any flour in it.
How can it feed the soul?
—Charles Spurgeon[1]

Let me take you back to the beginning: for many years I thought I was a good teacher. Then everything changed.

My gift was teaching interesting Sunday school lessons. I knew the Bible well and told its stories creatively so that younger kids looked forward to story time. Teens happily discussed Bible passages. Even adults would stop by to sit in on my classes. My lessons had a point too. I would build to a climactic moment that taught about living for God. I led discussions applying it to daily life. Kids left with practical instruction they could put to work in the coming week.

Every so often I would teach about how Jesus died for our sins. For those lessons the practical point would be the need to accept him as Savior. Even without asking for on-the-spot decisions, this was sometimes awkward. There was the pressure of the topic, the need to be inviting but not pushy—and always the eerie sadness of the cross itself. But I prayed extra hard before those lessons, hunkered down, and taught them.

I felt good about my "ministry niche" and wouldn't have changed a thing. But then God let me hear about Joe.

Joe was a fellow teacher who seemed smart enough, but bland—not the type who might captivate a group of kids. Yet Joe began teaching large-group lessons like I was doing. Others who saw him teach liked his lessons. They told me I might like them too. By the third time someone told me how good Joe was, I felt threatened. So I took the bait.

I decided to sit in on one of Joe's lessons. I took a seat in the back of the room and reminded myself to be neither jealous nor smug—to resist comparing his teaching with mine—but I couldn't help it. I was hoping I'd watch Joe teach and then be able to reassure myself I was still top dog in my teaching circle.

LEARNING FROM JOE

Joe's lesson was about Samuel, who was still a boy when God called him to be a prophet. I recognized it as an ideal lesson for any storyteller. It's about a child, so kids can relate, and the story builds to a nice climax. God calls repeatedly to Samuel at night. Samuel trots off each time to Eli the priest, whom he thinks must be the one calling. Eli eventually figures out what's happening and tells Samuel to respond and listen to God.

The Samuel story offers an opportunity to teach about being a good listener. Samuel listened, and God did great things through him. How could our students listen at home? At school? On the playground? What might God do if they listened better? I settled in to observe Joe's lesson. I wondered which of these themes he'd draw out, and how.

Although Joe wasn't a dynamic speaker, I had to admit he set the stage well for Samuel's big moment. He explained how God was largely silent in the days before Samuel. The rulers in the land were inept and the priests corrupt. The last big-time prophet had died centuries before. The people needed God to bring justice, and they were hungry to hear him speak.

Joe had a reason for that setup. To my surprise, his lesson didn't focus on Samuel's effort to listen but on God's desire to call out. Joe mentioned how God actually came and stood near Samuel's bed while calling his name. I'd never noticed that. And Joe discussed with the kids how God called with such a normal voice that Samuel was sure it must be Eli.

Joe was excited at how, after all that waiting, God's voice of justice came gently, personally, and humanlike to a child. "What does that tell you about God?" Joe asked. To show how God still speaks personally and humanly, he then read from Hebrews 1:1–2: "Long ago, at many times and in many ways, God spoke to our fathers by the prophets, but in these last days he has spoken to us by his Son."

By his *Son*? Joe was turning the lesson toward Jesus. I was impressed. It was a gutsy move I wouldn't have dared try. Bringing up Jesus when he wasn't already in the story always felt uncomfortable to me. But Joe pressed on. He said that Jesus came down and spoke too. Jesus taught us in ways no other prophet could. He showed us the face of God by walking among us and laughing with us, by scolding bullies and casting out demons, by looking into our sad eyes with tears in his own.

Most of all, Jesus spoke by dying on the cross. By bringing both justice and love to us in this way, he spoke the most beautiful word anyone could. Centuries before, God had left heaven to stand beside Samuel. In Jesus, God left all that glory to live beside you and me, and to die in place of you and me.

Now, Joe said, Jesus is risen. He gives his Spirit to speak to our hearts, in words soft enough to melt us and packed with the power we need to obey. God has spoken and he continues to speak—like never before.

A Taste of Jesus

I'm probably making Joe's lesson sound smoother than it actually was. Frankly, he stumbled around a lot as he said all this. His delivery was dry. Some of the kids got fidgety. Still, I sensed his focus on Jesus was the right way to teach the Bible, and I waited for the sales pitch—the part about accepting Jesus as Savior. But Joe never went there. He said a prayer—a real prayer asking that what we learned about Jesus would touch our hearts—and he was done.

Where was the application? Wasn't he at least going to tell the kids how to listen like Samuel? No. Gradually, I saw that Joe's chief purpose was just to let us see Jesus a little bigger and better than we'd seen him before.

Joe did lead a discussion to help the kids connect what they learned to life on the playground. He suggested that when they're the target of unkind words they might remember how God spoke to Samuel, and how richly Jesus had spoken to them. This would help them respond in a godly way to mean talk. But it was more about the heart than it was a rule.

It was good for Joe to make that connection. And it worked because, before Joe ever got to that point, his lesson had already begun stirring kids' hearts—and mine. It worked because the cross of Jesus—not principles for good living—is the engine of the Christian life. By simply getting a taste of Jesus, I was eager to listen to God in a way that wouldn't have happened if Joe had *told* me to listen. Joy in Jesus *was* the application!

To Know Nothing but Jesus

Joe understood Paul's message in 1 Corinthians 2:1–5, and he helped me to understand it as well.

> And I, when I came to you, brothers, did not come proclaiming to you the testimony of God with lofty speech or wisdom. For I decided to know nothing among you except Jesus Christ and him crucified. And I was with you in weakness and in fear and much trembling, and my speech and my message were not in plausible words of wisdom, but in demonstration of the Spirit and of power, so that your faith might not rest in the wisdom of men but in the power of God.

Paul's statement that he decided to teach *nothing* but Jesus and the cross is a jaw-dropper. *Nothing* else? Does he really mean that? If he does, then the implications for our own teaching are profound. Consider three things this passage tells us.

First, the content of the message matters; it must be about Jesus. Corinth was a stopping point for traveling sages who spouted wisdom about personal success and religious insight. Paul would not be one of them. His message about the cross of Christ was so superior that he spoke it plainly—weakly, he says, with trembling. He let the cross itself do the talking.

We shouldn't take this to mean that lively presentations are bad. Joe might have benefited from a more engaging style. But he got the main thing right. Joe had the same single-mindedness Paul had. What mattered was Christ crucified. Joe determined that his time with the kids would revolve around Jesus, and he pushed other considerations aside. He understood that those kids had school teachers or Sesame Street to tell them how to be good listeners. They needed *him* to show them something better—how Christ speaks so stunningly that listening will never be the same.

Second, the cross of Christ applies to the entire Christian life. It isn't just something you believe to become a Christian. It's also the framework for living *as* a Christian. Paul stayed in Corinth for a year and a half and spent that time teaching—just the cross. Perhaps after a while the Corinthian believers told Paul they were ready for new material. They knew this cross stuff. He could move on. But the beauty of Jesus's cross is so vast one could spend a lifetime catching just a fraction of it.

In fact, Paul did address a variety of topics in the church at Corinth. In 1 Corinthians alone, he gives instructions about bickering, sexual sin, marriage—even hairstyles. Does this mean he's exaggerating when he says Christ is his only message? No. It means that the most powerful way to handle *every* sin in the life of the church is to apply a deeper understanding of the cross of Christ.

If Joe's lesson had included God's call to initial belief in Jesus, that would have been okay. But by teaching the cross of Jesus without that invitation, Joe did something powerful. He treated the cross as ongoing fuel, even for kids who were already Christians.

Third, faith in this message comes from God. There's every reason to speak God's message God's way—because it's God who brings true repentance and spiritual growth.

Here lies the real reason I didn't make the cross the theme of my own lessons: I thought it felt corny. I didn't want to try too hard to be spiritual when I should be, well, more normal. I thought I knew what would work best with the kids I taught, and *what would make me look wise.* Although I claimed to rely on God, I feared entrusting my teaching to his ideas and the Holy Spirit's tools.

The message of Jesus's death and resurrection is a tool of the Spirit to change hearts. Nagging is not. Rather than coax the kids into temporarily *acting* better, Joe told about Jesus and trusted God to use that message to make the kids *become* better.

EUANGÉLION

In Bible times, the Greek word for "good news" or "gospel" (*euangélion*) was not a religious word. It was used for good news brought by a herald—perhaps news of a battle won or a king crowned—something everyone needed to hear and respond to. Jesus and the New Testament writers latched onto this word and used it to express the core of Christianity.

In Luke, *euangélion* is the approach God takes to the arrival of Jesus. The angel's announcement to the shepherds is: "I bring you good news (*euangélion*) of great joy" (Luke 2:10). Luke goes on to use the word more than twenty times in the books of Luke and Acts.

In Mark, *euangélion* is the first thing out of the gate: "Jesus came into Galilee, proclaiming the gospel of God, and saying, 'The time is fulfilled, and the kingdom of God is at hand; repent and believe in the gospel'" (Mark 1:14–15). This may be the most concise summary of Jesus's teaching in the Bible, and it's all about *euangélion.*

Paul uses some form of *euangélion* more than seventy times in his epistles. "Good news" is the central expression that powers the church.

How Christians Are Different

What should we make of this? Well, for sure we must not treat the good news as if it were a typical religion. Typical religion is about doing what your god or gods require; it's following your beliefs and methods to achieve some goal or approval. This is true whether you're offering pagan sacrifices in an ancient temple or seeking enlightenment through meditation. You *do* something to *earn* something.

Let's face it: Christianity is often packaged this way. Live a good life and things will go well for you. Find the right spiritual resources and you'll be blessed. Ask Jesus into your heart and you'll be saved. This is why many people say all religions are the same. In some sense, they're right.

But Jesus didn't bring typical religion. He brought *good news.*

I used to work in a television newsroom. Our best stories were always those with an immediate effect on our viewers' lives. For example, if there's a heavy snowstorm, it will almost always lead off a local newscast. The principle is, "Here's what's happened, and it will change your life." News is not what *you* do—it's what someone else has done that affects you.

The good news means you relate to God based on what *Jesus* has done for you, not what you've done to prove yourself worthy. If you're a believer, the good news says that God already accepts you fully—he's adopted you as his child—because you're joined to Jesus, who died on the cross for you.

Yes, believing this means a changed life. Flat out. You'll have a hungry, iron grip on Jesus. You'll run after him forcefully. But you'll do it because you rest in him. All your effort to obey will be a response to what he's already done, never a performance to win his favor. There's no need for such scheming. No pressure. No false fronts.

The typical lesson for kids isn't like this. Instead, it tends to be what mine were for years—little more than a lecture about some way you ought to live for God. Such lessons create pressure and invite pretending.

We've been dispensing good advice instead of the good news. Eventually, kids will tire of our advice, no matter how good it might be. Many will leave the church. Others will live decent, churchy lives but without any fire for Christ. We'll wonder why they've rejected the good news, because we assumed they were well grounded in it. In fact, they never were. Although we told stories of Jesus and his free grace, we watered it down with self-effort—and *that's* what they heard.

Fellow teachers, our challenge is to proclaim the good news of Jesus so clearly and consistently that no kid of ours will ever place him in a category with typical religious leaders. Our calling is to be good-news fanatics. I stress this because if I don't, someone will hear me talk of teaching about Jesus and get the wrong idea. They will think, "Yes, we ought to teach kids to be like Jesus and to follow his example." This would be *typical* religion.

What a tyrant Jesus would be if he lived a perfect life and then, as his main message, told us to be like him. What a setup for failure! What discouragement and worry would mark our lives! What masquerades they would be! We must understand that our central hope is in Jesus's *full* saving work, not just his instructions, and that kids will be stuck in the pressure-filled mode of trying to measure up unless we bombard them with this *good news*.

One more thing about the good news: when it comes to teaching it, all of us are clumsy. We all begin life inclined to try to earn our way before God. We all must learn to teach against our first instincts.

QUESTIONS YOU MIGHT BE ASKING

Why shouldn't I just follow the lesson points in my teacher's manual, or read my kids a children's devotional? Don't the folks who publish those materials know better than I do what kids need to hear?

Some published lessons are better than others. If you search, you can find several with good stuff. But few teachers always follow them straight through. Most of us use them as starting points and then pick and choose what works for us. We change things and add our own insights and activities that seem right. We chat with kids about what matters to us and about what we know matters to them. Good teaching is personal. If you use published material, make the good news the guide by which you tailor your lessons.

But what if I add something about Jesus and get it wrong?

An eager teacher who puts extra thought into a lesson—and shares what he or she's learned about Jesus—beats a timid one every time. You're right that if you try often enough to be Jesus-centered, you might eventually teach something half-baked. We should work hard to avoid that, and the second section of this book will help. But it still could happen. That's okay. The greater error is to teach from the Bible and fail to point out Jesus at all.

Wouldn't it be better to say we should be God-centered? Aren't you leaving out whole chunks of teaching about God by focusing only on Jesus?

The disciples said the same thing—to Jesus's face! "'Lord, show us the Father, and it is enough for us.' Jesus said to him, 'Whoever has seen me has seen the Father. How can you say, "Show us the Father"? Do you not believe that I am in the Father and the Father is in me?'" (John 14:8–10). Although we look to the entire Bible for a full picture of God, the most complete picture we find is Jesus himself. The Bible tells us "the light of the knowledge of the glory of God [is seen] in the face of Jesus Christ" (2 Corinthians 4:6). A focus on Jesus *is* God-centered. Plus, to love Jesus is the godliest activity imaginable. The Father has loved the Son perfectly, for eternity. Loving Jesus isn't ignoring the Father—it's imitating him. The theologian John Owen put it this way: "Nothing renders us so like unto God as our love unto Jesus Christ, for he is the principle object of his love; in him doth his soul rest, in him he is always well pleased."[2]

Did I read you right? Did you say "Ask Jesus into your heart and you'll be saved" is not *the good news?*

Kids *do* need to respond to Jesus in faith, and the call to do so is part of the good news. But the good news is also more than just

"Ask Jesus." We too easily turn faith into little requirements—like saying a certain prayer—that end up being all about something external *we* must do. On Pentecost, Peter preached the good news of what *Jesus* has done (using the Old Testament like Joe did, I might add). He didn't immediately ask for a behavioral response, but first let that good news lead to a heart response: "Now when they heard this they were cut to the heart, and said to Peter and the rest of the apostles, 'Brothers, what shall we do?'" (Acts 2:37) Only then did Peter tell his listeners to repent and be baptized, as a necessary part of what God was already working in them. I'll say more about how the good news works in nonbelievers in chapter 3.

It seems to me that Samuel is a good example of a kid who listened. Why shouldn't I teach that?

You could. There's nothing wrong with that. The Bible *does* give us useful examples. However, all too often that's all kids get from a lesson, instead of what they need most. If they get Samuel the good listener without first appreciating God the Great Speaker, they're liable to end up relating to God only in an anxious, what-I-must-do way. Joe's discussion time about how the lesson applied to life on the playground was important. It showed how God's speech to Samuel three thousand years ago matters to Jesus's followers today, and it encouraged the kids to believe and act on it. It's good to challenge kids to obey God. Just make sure they're responding out of faith in the love of Jesus, not out of mere moralism.

You also wouldn't have to emphasize God's speaking at all. There are other themes in the Samuel story, like God's determination to end injustice or his provision of a good king (the broader theme of the whole book of 1 Samuel), and these too would make fine lessons that lead to Jesus. I'll explain how to create such lessons in chapter 6.

The way Joe taught the Samuel story just seems too hard to me. I could never come up with all that.

You don't have to. Joe was actually a very experienced teacher with much practice. It's okay to start small. Begin by mentioning just one or two ways the good news of Jesus applies to each lesson you teach. In time, build on that. Remember, even Paul didn't think he spoke the good news particularly well. The power is in the message. If you know the good news of Jesus and dare to tell it, you are supremely gifted to advance God's kingdom—no matter how well you speak.

SHOW THEM JESUS RIGHT AWAY

It's good to take action immediately, while you're thinking about it. How can you apply these ideas right now? You might pick one or more of the suggestions from the list below:

Teachers: Pick a specific spot to talk about the cross of Jesus in your next lesson, discussion session, worship time, or whatever you lead. Besides helping your students see Jesus, this will accomplish two things: (1) you'll get used to looking for ways to connect the cross to every part of Christian life, and (2) you'll get comfortable talking about the cross, which sometimes feels weird until we get used to it. Be deliberate about doing this in every session you lead—*every one!*—until you've done it so much that talking about how Jesus died for us feels easy and natural.

Find another teacher who's committed to showing kids Jesus in every lesson. Arrange to sit in on a class. Afterward, note the things that teacher did to teach the good news—things you can learn from. Remember not to critique what the other teacher does wrong but to learn from what he or she gets right, and to let that teacher know what you appreciated!

Parents: If you feel uncomfortable talking with your kids about how Jesus died for us, start changing that right now by building a habit of mentioning the cross. Work it into family devotions, discussions in the car, or whatever you like. If you can't settle on any other specific time to mention it, simply add it to regular prayers at mealtime or bedtime. Pray something like: "Father, thank you for giving your Son Jesus to die for our sins." You can adjust the wording, but say the prayer *daily,* and engage in other Jesus discussions until talk of the cross becomes natural and no longer feels weird in your home.

Grandparents: If you don't see your grandkids regularly, write each of them a letter. Like Paul's letter to the Corinthians, make sure it says something about Jesus. Kids love getting mail, and they'll especially love getting a letter from *you!*

Anyone: Consider using the story of the boy Samuel (1 Samuel 3) to guide your personal devotions for a few days. Do it in three steps.

1. *Notice* ways God acts in the story. There are more than I mentioned in this chapter, so you might want to write them down.
2. *Meditate* on ways Jesus acts the same in the New Testament, as well as today, and thank him for the kind of Savior he is.
3. *Share.* The next time you're alone with your kids or have a few extra minutes in class, share about your time studying Samuel and what you learned. Let your kids observe your own desire to see Jesus.

Chapter 2
The God Report Card
Because the good news is like nothing else

This is the great mystery of the gospel
in the blood of Christ, that those who sin every day
should have peace with God all their days.
—John Owen[1]

It was the Sunday after Christmas, and the group I taught was typical for that week. Many students were gone. Some who remained had relatives visiting and brought their cousins to Sunday school.

One of these visitors was a middle schooler named Nicole. She seemed comfortable being in church. She joined in our prayer circle and knew some of the worship songs. In the weeks leading up to Christmas, we'd studied the birth of Jesus from Luke, and as I reviewed those lessons, Nicole was eager to share what she knew about those stories. I figured she probably had a decent grasp of the good news—after all, she was a church kid.

THE ONLY ONE WHO OBEYED
For our post-Christmas lesson we were continuing in Luke with the story of Jesus's visit to Jerusalem as a twelve-year-old. By this time I'd learned to teach the good news every week, so I started by reminding the kids how characters in the birth narrative called baby Jesus the Savior, the Son of God, and the eternal King who brings forgiveness.

Then I asked, "But do you know what Jesus himself said? Does anyone know the first thing the Bible mentions Jesus saying about why he came?"

The answer, of course, is in the story of Jesus's visit to Jerusalem with his parents. As they headed home he was missing. They searched three days before finding him in the temple, where we get his first recorded words: "Did you not know that I must be in my Father's house?" (Luke 2:49). That comment is packed with meaning. Jesus wasn't just referring to the temple. To be in his Father's house meant to be employed by his Father. To obey. To do—and finish—the work the Father sent him to do.

Jesus went home with his parents "and was submissive to them" (Luke 2:51). As for obeying God, the cost becomes clear as Luke's Gospel unfolds. On his last visit to Jerusalem, Jesus again failed to leave. Rather than flee danger, he went just a few steps beyond its walls to the one place where he knew soldiers would come to capture him— Gethsemane. There he prayed to his Father, "Not my will, but yours, be done" (Luke 22:42).

I included all this in my lesson to show the big picture. Luke didn't write about Jesus the twelve-year-old to give my kids an example they could relate to and follow. Rather, Luke paints a portrait of a Savior who submits so completely to God—both to God's law and to God's plan of redemption through the cross—that we can only watch in wonder. The main point is not that we too should obey, but that Jesus *did* obey.

I thought it was a clever lesson, but Nicole just looked puzzled. I explained how we often fail to obey our parents and God, but how as Christians we can still be confident, happy, and eager to obey the next time. I explained that this is because we belong to Jesus, who did obey and died in our place to make our lives pleasing to God. I thought that would help.

I was wrong. For Nicole, the idea that Jesus's obedience could have any bearing on what God thinks of *her* just didn't make sense. "That's crazy," she finally said.

I sat there for a while, not sure what to say. Then I remembered that in my box of teaching supplies I had an object lesson that might help. I asked the kids to wait while I dug around for it. Sure enough, there was the God Report Card.

First, a Warning

I'll get back to Nicole's story later in this chapter. First, I need to more fully explain what I mean by the "good news."

Let me start with a warning: The good news offends everyone. At some point it will offend *you*. It might be the gruesomeness of the cross. It might be the absolute freeness of salvation, or how that includes giving up your self-directed life. It may be something else entirely. But if you're honest, at some point you'll say, "Wait, *I don't like this*."

Paul made this very point: "Jews demand signs and Greeks seek wisdom, but we preach Christ crucified, a stumbling block to Jews and folly to Gentiles, but to those who are called, both Jews and Greeks, Christ the power of God and the wisdom of God" (1 Corinthians 1:22–24).

First-century Jews and Greeks are long gone, but we know their types. The Greeks were worldly-wise; they considered themselves smarter than people of backwoods religions, where blood sacrifice ruled the day. The cross violated their enlightened sensibilities. That God would send his Son to die was folly—primitive and senseless. How would *that* help you get ahead in the world?

The Jews, on the other hand, didn't mind sacrifices but wouldn't let go of their demanding self-righteousness and their trust in religious observances. "Why? Because they did not pursue it by faith, but as if it were based on works" (Romans 9:32). The Jews insisted on the need to *do something* to impress God.

Most churchgoers I know give the cross lip service, but deep down they're like either the Greeks or the Jews. To "Greeks," the cross is an embarrassment. It's about sin and the wrath of God and the way we must obey a deity who makes all the rules. Wouldn't it be healthier to avoid such negative talk? To "Jews," the cross is dangerous. It's about a frightening idea that sometimes our fancy prayers and religious works only serve to keep us distant from God. The idea that God wipes out a lifetime of sin at the cross—with no contribution at all from our churchy habits—makes us squirm. After all, if all the work was done at the cross, how could we compare ourselves to others and still come out on the narrow road?

For both groups, the cross is best kept on the margins. It's uncomfortable. Scandalous.

In light of all this, we might downplay the cross. Then we wouldn't offend anyone. For years I tiptoed around the cross for this very reason. But this offends the good news itself. I'm beginning to see that God designed the cross to shock absolutely *everyone*.

So, you've been warned. One test that you're teaching the true good news is that you've personally had to struggle with its insult. Another is that sooner or later someone—perhaps even a "pillar of the church"—will hear about what you're teaching and complain.

What Is the Good News?

The good news encompasses so much, but the opening verses of 1 Corinthians 15 give a helpful summary.

> Now I would remind you, brothers, of the gospel I preached to you, which you received, in which you stand, and by which you are being saved, if you hold fast to the word I preached to you— unless you believed in vain. For I delivered to you as of first importance what I also received: that Christ died for our sins in accordance with the Scriptures, that he was buried, that he was raised on the third day in accordance with the Scriptures. (1 Corinthians 15:1–4)

Let's frame our discussion around the essence of what Paul says is "of first importance"—the simple phrase, "Christ died for our sins." We'll drill into the core of the good news in three steps:

1. Christ
2. Died
3. For our sins.

The good news is about Jesus Christ.

It's real news about the eternal Son of God who became a living, breathing person named Jesus, who died and rose again and still lives today. If we keep reading in 1 Corinthians 15, we will see Paul mention person after person who saw Jesus in the flesh after his resurrection.

Jesus's death and resurrection is more than a poignant idea that helps us love God. It indeed gives us love, but this is because the cross is the actual loving act that kindles our own love, and Jesus is the real and risen Savior who rescues all who are his.

He's the sort of man who powerfully hushed the most violent storm with a word and then, on the next page, lovingly touched the festering skin of a leper. He told religious blowhards they were sons of the devil and told prostitutes they were forgiven. He raised the dead and directed the praise for it away from himself. Remarkable.

Jesus's title, Christ, means "anointed." Priests, prophets, and kings were all anointed in biblical times. Jesus too is our priest, our go-between with the Father, but it doesn't stop there. He's also the supreme prophet and teacher from whom we learn the mysteries of God. And he's our Creator King, the eternal guardian to whom we owe all allegiance. He is wisdom incarnate, the Good Shepherd, Lord of lords and King of kings. *That guy* died for our sins.

The good news is about Jesus's death and resurrection.

This is a narrow definition, given how the good news soaks absolutely every part of Christian life. But narrow is helpful; it ensures that the cross and the resurrection remain our focus, even when we broaden our spotlight to take in more.

All of God's saving work is connected. This means that the good news includes some critical things that happened long *before* the cross.

God chose us in Jesus "before the foundation of the world" (Ephesians 1:4). Salvation was already at work in the Old Testament's stories, laws, prophesies, and wisdom—so in a broad sense this all might be called good news. Yet we don't get a clear announcement until the angels visit the shepherds and Jesus begins his ministry, and we don't see it fully realized until the cross.

Likewise, Jesus's victory is applied to us *after* the resurrection in ways we mustn't forget when considering the scope of the good news. He ascended to heaven to advocate and reign for us. We have adoption as sons, Spirit-enabled holiness, and future glory. But all of these flow from Jesus's finished work on the cross. This is why I often speak of the good news in the more narrow sense, which Paul says is "of first importance." It's usually helpful to think of our ongoing good works, in particular, as separate from the good news itself. Even as we give our lives for God's kingdom, this is only an echo of the life Jesus gave.

The good news is that Jesus died for our sins.

Jesus lived a perfect life and had no sin of his own to condemn him, but he took our place as a substitute. This means that although we still sin, *at the same time* we can also be completely accepted and loved by a holy God who hates sin.

A good-news teacher must not sugarcoat God's demands. The Bible describes sin as our willful rebellion against God and all that's delightful in the universe. God is Father, Son, and Spirit—each person loving the others. He created us to reflect that love and to care for his good world. But we chose self-interest and self-effort above the beauty of God, spurning our Creator. Our adultery stunk up his world. If I had a dead skunk in my house, it would be good for me to get rid of it. In the same way, God would have been right to destroy us.

But God didn't destroy us. Instead, in all the torments of sin Jesus took our place.

- *Sin means we were doomed to die. But Jesus died to give us eternal life.* "[He] died for us so that whether we are awake or asleep we might live with him" (1 Thessalonians 5:10).

- *Sin means we were cursed. But Jesus became cursed to make us blessed.* "Christ redeemed us from the curse of the law by becoming a curse for us" (Galatians 3:13).

- *Sin means we were shamed. But Jesus endured the shame of the cross to give us honor.* "He has now reconciled [you] in his body of flesh by his death, in order to present you holy and blameless and above reproach before him" (Colossians 1:22).

- *Sin means we were guilty. But Jesus was condemned and punished so we could be declared not guilty,* "canceling the record of debt that stood against us with its legal demands. This he set aside, nailing it to the cross" (Colossians 2:14).

- *Sin means we were enemies of God and deserving of his anger. But Jesus deflected that wrath onto himself to give us God's favor.* "While we were enemies we were reconciled to God by the death of his Son" (Romans 5:10).

- *Sin means we were shut out from fellowship with God. But Jesus died alone on the cross so we might never be lonely again.* "For Christ also suffered once for sins, the righteous for the unrighteous, that he might bring us to God" (1 Peter 3:18).

- *Sin means we had no hope of lasting happiness. But Jesus suffered sadness to give us eternal joy.* "Surely he has borne our griefs and carried our sorrows" (Isaiah 53:4).

Now we who were spiritual stinkers, unable to please God, are set free to serve a risen Savior. "He died for all, that those who live might no longer live for themselves but for him who for their sake died and was raised" (2 Corinthians 5:15). It's a stunning turnaround.

And the reason? God's reason for giving his only Son to be punished, killed, spurned, shamed, and so on is that *he loves us.* The same love the Father has for the Son—that eternal, perfect, fatherly love—God extends to us.

THE KID WHO CRIED

Knowing we're saved is critical. If we somehow think we never were in hellish danger, we might still admire Jesus, but we won't love him.

I once was teaching a group of kindergartners when the topic turned to how we sometimes get angry. One student commented loudly that Jesus said anyone who gets angry will go to hell. I confirmed that Jesus did say something like that.

Well, another little boy started to cry. I felt terrible. I was sure I'd allowed too much about sin and judgment. What to do? I had just enough sense to turn the discussion to the good news. I said, "Yes, Jesus did say if you get angry for a bad reason you deserve for God to punish you. But Jesus never got angry for a bad reason. So who deserves to be punished, you or Jesus?"

"We do," they said.

"But who *did* get punished? Who died on the cross?" I asked.

"Jesus."

"That's right," I said. "Jesus already got the punishment. So if you belong to Jesus, even if you get angry, God won't punish you. It wouldn't be fair to punish you because Jesus already got punished instead."

The little boy who'd been crying looked up. For a few seconds he studied me to see if I was serious. Then he grinned. A huge grin. The kind of smile that nearly made *me* cry.

It was one of those rewarding moments that makes years of teaching worthwhile, and it never would have happened if I'd merely been teaching that Jesus died for us. The boy had heard that line before. But because this time he'd experienced a sharper conviction of his sin in the face of God's holiness—a *need* to be saved—the good news brought joy. That smile was worship. Jesus became bigger to him.

HOW TO STAND LIKE A CHRISTIAN

The good news isn't just about escaping punishment. It's also new life. Our 1 Corinthians 15 passage says we must *hold fast* to it. Once it's preached and received, it becomes the gospel *in which you stand*. In Jesus, we have status to stand before God, doing his bidding and enjoying his care. Notice how this is current. Day by day we continue to stand in the good news. It has ongoing value.

Even though the good news is what Jesus has done—not anything we do—as we believe it, it compels us to action. Paul explains it this way: "For by grace you have been saved through faith. And this is not your own doing; it is the gift of God, not a result of works, so that no one may boast. For we are his workmanship, created in Christ Jesus for good works, which God prepared beforehand, that we should walk in them" (Ephesians 2:8–10).

Our salvation is generous and full. Yes, we're saved by grace alone—but God knows we not only need to be loved in spite of our stench, but also to become non-stinkers. He includes as part of salvation our rebirth into people who erupt in true worship of our Savior—with good works.

We are *created in Christ Jesus.* Joined to him by faith, we can do what formerly was unthinkable. We begin to do truly selfless works. They aren't worth a cent for earning God's love; but because we're in Christ, God finds us pleasing. He accepts our bumbling acts done in thankfulness as offerings to him. We're redeemed that we "might serve him without fear, in holiness and righteousness before him all our days" (Luke 1:74–75).

The good news heals, and then it empowers. It makes us eager to serve God and our neighbor. As the Holy Spirit grows it within us, showing us more and more what standing and power we have in Jesus, the good news continues to renew us as long as we live. It's what teachers everywhere hope for their students.

IF GOD GAVE GRADES

Nicole and the other kids from the beginning of this chapter couldn't understand why Jesus's obedience should matter to them. It sounded like a bit of doctrine with little impact on daily life—a lame lesson.

I got a manila envelope out of my teaching box and showed it to the kids. On it was printed "Report Card" and under that a line for a name. I wrote "me" on the line.

"Imagine this is your report card and you have to show it to God," I told them. "Instead of schoolwork, you earn grades in five godly subjects: obeying your parents, generosity, kindness, telling the truth, and putting yourself last. What grades do you think you've earned?"

A few kids thought they might have As in a subject or two. Most told me what I've heard from hundreds of kids over the years—they thought they should get Bs and Cs. Nicole was particularly interested in the question, assigning herself a range of grades from a B+ in kindness to a D in generosity. "I like my stuff too much," she explained. "I know God wants me to be more generous."

"I get that way too," I told her. "But I'm glad you can see that God is strict. In fact, he's so strict that no matter how well we do, every one of us earns exactly the same grades from God."

I opened the envelope and pulled out the report card. Next to each spiritual subject, written in dark marker, was a large F.

Some kids were surprised. So I explained that God is so holy that we have to be perfect. Anything less is an F. "What would it be like for you to bring home all Fs on a real report card?" I asked.

The kids said they'd be discouraged. They'd be scared of their parents' anger and of punishment. One boy even said his dad might stop picking him up from school. "Someone might see me getting in his car," he said, "and if they knew about the Fs, they'd think we were a bad family."

That admission made us somber. We talked about how shame is one result of our sin. "But the good news is that God fixes our sin problem," I said. "Does anyone know what he does?"

"He forgives us?" someone suggested.

"Yes," I said. "That's like erasing all our Fs. But could he do something even better? If I erased all the Fs on this report card, what would I have left?"

"A blank report card."

"That's right," I said. "And I wouldn't feel good about a blank report card either. I'd have to work very hard to try to earn some good grades so it wouldn't be blank anymore. That's what happens when we think that God only forgives us. We still feel impossible pressure to do good things to make him happy."

"God could give us all As."

"Now you're getting somewhere," I said. "But an A doesn't mean anything unless someone earned it. And we aren't good enough to earn As. So where's an A going to come from?" The kids didn't know. They were out of ideas.

"Okay, let me show you the good news," I said. I reached into my box and pulled out a second report card. This one had "Jesus" printed on the envelope.

"Jesus lived a perfect life," I said. "He earned an A+ in everything." Then I opened the Jesus envelope and pulled out his report card, marked with an A+ in every subject. I took that card and put it in the envelope marked "me." Then I took the card with all the Fs and put it in the envelope marked "Jesus."

The Protest

"Nuh-uh! You can't do that!" It was Nicole.

"Jesus and I just traded report cards," I told her. "Why don't you like that?"

"You can't do that to him," she told me. "It's wrong."

I was expecting this. Nearly every time I've revealed the solution to the God Report Card, some students have protested. Often they don't like how easy it is to get all As. In this case, Nicole's main concern was with the other side of the equation. She was bothered by Jesus getting the Fs.

I asked, "Haven't you ever heard that Jesus died for your sins?"

She had, of course. But as Nicole tried to explain, it became clear she'd always imagined a noble Jesus bravely going to the cross to die. Now she was hit with the idea that Jesus took on something more—something like coming home with a bad report card and getting punished, feeling disgrace, and receiving anger he didn't deserve. "It's embarrassing for him," she explained.

"Yes, it was," I agreed. "Lots of people have died for someone else. But no one has come close to doing as much as Jesus did for you. Jesus didn't deserve to be punished—his resurrection proves that—but on the cross, he got whatever *you* deserve. Even your shame. He took it all."

Nothing to Earn

Nicole still wanted to know why I seemed happy to teach that Jesus got Fs. So I turned the discussion to her feelings about God. "I notice you worship and pray," I told her. "Why do you do those things?"

"Sometimes it's fun," she answered, "but mostly because it's good. God wants you to. Even when it's not so fun, I feel better afterwards."

"Well, I'm glad you worship and pray," I said. "But it sounds like you're mostly doing it to get God to like you. You feel good about yourself when you do well—and guilty when you don't." Nicole agreed.

"So let's talk about how we'd feel if we knew we had a report card that was already all A+'s," I said.

The kids told me they'd no longer be scared at all. One girl was sure her parents would reward her with ice cream. I suggested that since the good marks all came from Jesus, the kids might work hard to add a few marks they'd actually earned so they could be proud of what *they'd* done. But they all understood that would be foolish, and disrespectful of what Jesus had given them.

"Good," I said. "Now you understand one of the big ways Christians are different from everyone else. We Christians get our good record—the Bible calls it 'righteousness'—from God. It doesn't come from what we do. Lots of people try to stop being bad. But Christians also stop trying to prove how good they are."

It was time for class to end, so I turned and spoke to Nicole. "If you're joined to Jesus, God is pleased with you. Like he is with Jesus. Like you obey *that* perfectly. Of course you still have a duty to actually obey God, but it's not the kind of duty that comes because you need to keep him from getting grumpy. It's the kind of higher duty that comes from being loved, and in love. Only the righteousness you get from

Jesus will ever make you completely, *perfectly* accepted, like getting all A+'s. No more shame.

"Believe it. Believe that you're safe in Jesus. Believe that his love for you doesn't change. The more you believe this, the less you'll pray and read the Bible and worship because you're scared you have to. You'll do it because you *want* to."

Nicole nodded seriously. I could tell she got it, though I think she found it hard to believe. That's okay—the good news *is* unbelievably good. I gave her a smile and dismissed everyone.

Nothing Better

The God Report Card is a rich illustration. It helps clarify how a life based on Christ's death for our sins is better than any of the lesser ways we might be tempted to approach God:

It's better than moralism.

Merely trying to live a good life makes kids either proud or frustrated. But the good news allows for no pride, since we've done nothing to earn the righteousness we're given. Nor does it allow despair, since only Jesus had to measure up. Kids can be humble, yet supremely confident of God's approval.

It's better than grudging forgiveness.

It trumps the lie that God forgives us when necessary but still counts on us to do our best, looking down on us with frequent scowls. Like a blank report card, grudging forgiveness leaves kids anxious about living for God. The good news frees them to enjoy a life of service to a God who's on their side.

It's better than cheap grace.

It beats the notion of a coddling God who easily loves you as long as you're pretty good or you once said the right prayer—no problem for him, no further demands on you. Cheap grace sounds comforting, but God ends up irrelevant and boring. The good news shows how sin is deadly serious and required costly love from Jesus. It captures kids' hearts for a worthy God who rightly calls for whole-life repentance.

It's better than therapeutic religion.[2]

We too often think a Christian life means finding the right kind of prayer, worship, teaching, and other "Jesus stuff" that'll make us feel good or develop better habits. But the good news says that the Christian experience is a complete change of being. God has rescued us from death to life, and from shame to glory. This is far more motivating than self-improvement.

It's better than Jesus-as-example.

Doing good in the world, like Jesus did, is important. But Jesus-as-example alone gives kids no power to actually live in the self-sacrificing way Jesus modeled. Only when they're powered by the good news will they follow with abandon. Then there will be no stopping them.

The good news does not let Christianity become a guidebook by which kids adjust their lives. Adjustments are not enough, and bare rules are for flunkies who have no share in the family business. We are heirs of the King. We are reborn. We've emerged from catastrophe in a burst from God that leaves us stunned, exhilarated, and irreversibly transformed.

I wanted to say all this to Nicole. I'd only taught her one aspect of being joined to Jesus. I wanted to add how we're adopted, making it a thrill to obey the Father who loves and welcomes us. I could have told her how we're made holy so that we boldly live like the new people we are in Christ. I could have told her of eternal hope, and how the promise of resurrection drives us to serve God with eager expectation. Why not consider how *every part* of the good news is fuel for a confident Christian life?

Nicole was already heading down the hall with her cousins. I thought about chasing after them. Maybe we could talk more over lunch, their families and mine—but I stopped myself. They probably had plans. Besides, what middle schooler wants to spend her Christmas break listening to some teacher rant on about Jesus?

It would take too long to tell it all and fully convey the wonder. It would take a lifetime.

QUESTIONS YOU MIGHT BE ASKING

It sounds like you're saying it doesn't matter how we act as Christians. Don't we still have to work hard to obey God?

This is a common objection whenever our acceptance in Jesus is presented in all its scandalous freeness. It's as old as the Bible itself: "What shall we say then? Are we to continue in sin that grace may abound? By no means! How can we who died to sin still live in it?" (Romans 6:1–2) In no way is it okay to keep sinning. The idea that God's grace might let us go ahead and sin misses how big a change it is to become a Christian. That idea belongs to our old life with its get-away-with-sin attitude. We're reborn. We have a new life with new and better incentives to obey God.

But with the God Report Card, shouldn't you include something about how we need to accept Jesus in order to receive those "good grades"?

Often I do teach the need to respond in repentance and faith to the good news, but I didn't do it with this lesson for two reasons. First, I wanted to focus on what Jesus did for us because we easily obsess over what *we* must do—and then the good news gets lost. If the Holy Spirit gets through to a kid's heart, a proper response will follow without much coaxing from me. Second, the point of our discussion was that believing the good news is a critical habit even *after* becoming a Christian. The lesson wasn't about how to be saved. The God Report Card is about how kids who are already believers can gain confidence and joy by understanding the good news that they're justified before God.

To say Jesus is the only way to be saved sounds exclusive and dismissive of other religions. Are you sure Jesus is that special?

Yup. That insistence on Jesus is part of the scandal of the good news. The Bible is clear about it, so to say otherwise is dismissive toward the Bible. If it helps, remember that no other major religion claims a figure anything like him—the Son of God become human, suffering the consequences of our sin and rising from the dead. He really *is* unique. If you still aren't sure, carefully read Colossians 1:15–23 and ask yourself if such a human being fits any other religion you know.

You said little about the teachings of Jesus. Isn't what he taught just as important as what he did?

What Jesus taught is extremely important. I just don't want us to miss what he did. We must not separate his teaching from his saving work, which is foundational. Luke wrote "to compile a narrative of the things that have been accomplished among us" (Luke 1:1). Jesus is first of all about things *accomplished*. Both Luke and Matthew begin by telling why the coming Messiah is important: He'll save the people from their sins (Matthew 1:21). He'll reign forever and be the holy Son of God (Luke 1:32–35). He'll bring salvation from enemies (Luke 1:69–71). He'll be a Savior (Luke 2:11). Not a word about a great teacher coming. Jesus *is* a great teacher, of course—the best. Those who truly have him as their Savior also embrace him as their Teacher. Still, his teaching, like the rest of his life on earth, supports the central work of the cross.

If I used the God Report Card with my students, they'd have different responses than yours did. What do I do then?

Go with whatever is making an impact on your students. I find it's different every time. That's why we have that long list of the many problems Jesus solves by dying in our place. Any of them makes a fine talk about the good news. Nicole was impacted by the shame of the cross, so I used that as my angle.

Then what about all those other good news themes?

Use them next time—or the time after that. It's good to give kids many exposures to the good news from different starting points and angles. Every Bible story features a unique way that God cares for his people. If you find it and then teach the good news from that starting point, you'll constantly give your students new chances for the good news to click with them. You'll learn more about that later in this book.

I realize we have to acknowledge sin. But if I talk about it too much with the kids I teach, they just feel guilty and down on themselves. Are you sure that's a good idea?

Well, you've diagnosed those kids' core spiritual problem. Their true trust is in their own ability to act like good Christians, and your talk about sin exposes them as failures. Kids who trust in being good can't handle reminders of their sin. It destroys their self-confidence, precisely because it *is* confidence in self.

For those who firmly trust Jesus, even a hard look at their sin only makes them appreciate him more. The cure for kids who feel burdened by sin is not to ignore the topic (they feel the burden anyway, even if they aren't talking about it), but to administer large doses of the good news so that their trust in Jesus grows. We are sinners but no longer guilty, no longer unclean, no longer ashamed.

SHOW THEM JESUS RIGHT AWAY

You're ready now to make and teach with your own God Report Cards, or put what you've learned into action some other way. Here are a few ideas:

Parents: Use card paper and manila envelopes to make report cards for you and each of your children. You'll each need a blank envelope with a space to write a name on it, and a card inside that lists godly activities with blank spaces to give grades. Each of you will also need a second, filled-out envelope with Jesus's name on it and an identical card inside that lists those godly activities with grades of A+ already awarded—but keep those Jesus cards hidden at first.

1. Pass out the blank report cards and have each child write his or her name on it. Have them fill in whatever grades they think they've earned.

2. Discuss the grades they gave themselves. Explain God's demand for perfection, and have everyone change their grades to all Fs.

3. Discuss what a problem this is. Let the kids offer solutions (none of which is as good as God's solution).

4. Reveal God's solution by giving each child a Jesus Report Card. Tell how Jesus earned the A+'s we can't, and have the kids swap their cards with the ones for Jesus.

5. Talk about what the swap means for both Jesus and you. What did Jesus do for you? How is being freely forgiven and receiving righteousness from God different from *earning* our own righteousness? You might read 2 Corinthians 5:21, "For our sake he made him to be sin who knew so sin, so that in him we might become the righteousness of God."

Teachers: Make a set of God Report Cards (described for parents above) to keep with your teaching supplies. This way, you'll always have a teaching tool handy to bring out and demonstrate when your classroom discussions take a turn that calls for it. Or, if there's another illustration of the good news that you prefer, make yourself a visual aid for teaching that. But make sure you have *something*. It's much easier to launch into impromptu explanations of the good news when you have an illustration or prop ready to go at any time.

Teachers of younger kids: The God Report Card may be too abstract for kids under age eight or nine to grasp well. Try these alternatives to teach younger kids the same idea:

- *Younger elementary.* Use removable, nametag-sized stickers. Have kids write or draw pictures of sins they do on some of the stickers, and stick those sins onto their body or clothing. Have other stickers for Jesus. Write or draw pictures of the ways Jesus obeyed God's law (he helped hurting people, obeyed his parents, etc.) and stick those onto a piece of poster board with "Jesus" written on it. Talk about the difference between us and Jesus. Then swap stickers to show how he took our sin on himself and gives us his righteousness.

- *Preschool.* Play with puppets, dolls, or stuffed animals. Act out a situation where one of the puppets is naughty and has to be punished (like with a time-out). The other puppet does nothing wrong and deserves no punishment. Then have the innocent puppet volunteer to take the punishment the guilty puppet deserved. Talk about how Jesus did something like that for us. We deserve to be punished for how we disobey God; Jesus took our punishment in our place, even though he didn't deserve it.

Anyone: Get more familiar with the good news by doing a simple Bible study of some of the major benefits that come to you because you're joined to Jesus. Here's a list:

- *Justification.* You are declared "not guilty" and credited with Christ's righteousness (Romans 3:21–24).
- *Adoption.* You become a child of God (Romans 8:14–17).
- *Sanctification.* You more and more learn to live like the holy person you've already begun to be (Titus 2:11–15).
- *Glorification.* One day God's work for you, and in you, will be complete as you're made perfect (1 Corinthians 15:42–44).

Take one of these benefits at a time and consider two questions: (1) What does the passage say is wonderful about what I receive in Jesus? (2) How does this motivate me to live for Jesus? Be sure either to do this study with the kids you teach or to share afterward with them what you learned.

Chapter 3
The "Gospel Day" Trap
Because the good news is for church kids too

It is the end of our ministry
to bring the soul and Christ together;
and let no debts, no sins hinder.
—Richard Sibbes[1]

It was Sunday morning and snowing. There wasn't so much snow that church or Sunday school was canceled, but as I shoveled out my driveway, I realized there was enough that many families would stay home. Attendance would be low for my class.

I was disappointed. But when I got to church, I found Laura, a fellow teacher, even more bothered. Laura absolutely didn't want to waste her lesson on a day when only half her students would be there. As she scurried around to find something else to do with her class, she explained to me, "This was going to be 'gospel day.'"

I knew exactly what she meant. Laura is an excellent teacher who cares about her students' salvation. She knew some of them had already made a commitment to Jesus, but she wasn't sure about others. She figured they could use a nudge. At the very least, they needed to have God's plan of salvation and his call to believe presented to them clearly. So she resolved to take one day out of the year to do that.

But that morning, she was stuck. I recognized what had happened because I too have been there—in the "gospel-day" trap.

THE TRAP

The gospel-day trap happens when we think of the good news as very important—critical to salvation!—but as something that only some kids need to hear some of the time. There are two problems that result from this kind of thinking.

First, those few times each year that we "present the gospel" become artificial and forced. The kids feel pressure—and, as in Laura's case, so does the teacher. So instead of announcing the gospel with joy like the angel did to the shepherds, we use a tone that builds tension. The good news, which ought to make the heart glad, instead makes the stomach uncomfortable. By treating it as "special," we sabotage the chance for kids to receive it happily. Everyone quickly learns that the good news means pressure, and that other topics make for more fun groups and classes. That's the trap.

Second, this means church kids—those we assume are doing fine because they're from Christian homes and go to church—seldom hear the good news. For *any* message to make a life-changing impression usually takes hearing it again and again. This is doubly true with the good news because we all have a sinful nature inclined to prove ourselves rather than trust Jesus. Kids who only hear the good news a little tend to become kids who only love and trust Jesus a little.

I'm not saying that every day should be "gospel day." Rather, I'm suggesting an approach that makes such a day unnecessary. If we regularly weave the good news into *every* lesson, treating it as the one truth most practical and valuable for helping that day's topic come alive in us, we can avoid this trap.

Few of us would limit Bible reading or prayer to a few times a year. We know they're essential habits. Well, so is hearing and believing the good news. The kids we teach need it constantly.

Church kids come in one of two types—unsaved and saved. *Both types* desperately need to see Jesus. Let's consider first why unsaved kids need this.

ONE KIND OF CHURCH KID: UNSAVED

Many church kids may not be true believers. If you don't believe me just look at the evidence. True faith brings ongoing repentance and a new direction to life. But as with others in the church, many young people lead lives that are barely different from the culture at large. Instead of working to reorient their lives to a godly course, they fake just enough Christian behavior to get by.

Or they might actually love church. They might feel worshipful, witness to friends, go on missions trips, and lead prayer groups. But they do these things because being "churchy" feels good to them—not because of a saving relationship with God. Such kids may be fooled into thinking their behavior is true faith when, in fact, the reason for their religious fervor is rooted in themselves.

Any kid could be the one who needs to be saved. Much of the time, we just don't know.

In any case, recent studies showing that more than half of American church kids will drop out before age 30 should wake us up.[2] Many kids in our youth groups, Sunday school classes, Christian camps—or our homes—have never been irreversibly captured by the good news.

I don't bring this up to discourage you. Rather, I say it in the hope that it will cause us, in desperation, to look to God. He alone works salvation, and his mercy is abundant. We can have much hope for our kids if we rely on God and use his methods.

The True Decision-Maker

We learn this from Jesus's talk with Nicodemus. Nicodemus was a leading religious teacher and a careful follower of God who liked the signs he'd seen Jesus do. However, we can also detect some pride from how he opened the discussion. "Rabbi, we know that you are a teacher come from God, for no one can do these signs that you do unless God is with him" (John 3:2).

Jesus would have none of it. He answered Nicodemus bluntly, "Truly, truly, I say to you, unless one is born again he cannot see the kingdom of God" (John 3:3). Nicodemus thought he could see. He thought his learning and religious activities made him a good judge of what was spiritual. But Jesus used the imagery of being born to show him that his trust in religious deeds was actually keeping him from putting his faith where it should be—in God. Being born is not something you *do*; it's something that happens *to* you. No one can be truly spiritual unless the Spirit has worked in him, sprouting spiritual life.

Jesus continued, "The wind blows where it wishes, and you hear its sound, but you do not know where it comes from or where it goes. So it is with everyone who is born of the Spirit" (John 3:8). The Spirit works where *he* wishes. And everyone—even an upstanding church guy like Nicodemus—needs the new birth only God can fashion. This means we must toss aside our own salvation formulas.

We must not trust the "churchy behavior" formula. It's great to see a kid live a largely moral life and practice Christian disciplines. But God doesn't count that as obedience unless it flows from true faith in Jesus, which is prompted by the Spirit. "Without faith it is impossible to please him" (Hebrews 11:6).

We must not trust the "good family" formula. Yes, God works through families. I'm convinced there are true believers who grow up hearing the good news in Christian families and experience new birth and conversion so early in life they can't remember a time they didn't love Jesus. We can hope this for kids and pray for it. But it isn't automatic. God's work is absolutely necessary, and his timing is often later in a kid's life than we would choose.

We must not trust the "say-a-prayer" formula. Generations of church kids have been taught to become Christians by saying the "sinner's prayer." Certainly prayer is appropriate at the moment of conversion, but it's an empty incantation unless God's heart work has prompted it. The true decision-maker is God. Raising hands at Bible camp and walking down the aisle only counts if the Spirit has brought change on the inside.

If our tone shows the true basis of our trust to be in one of these formulas, that's what kids will trust too. We pronounce them saved—then they grow up and realize they *aren't* really changed. They give up on Christianity, and it's hard to bring them back. They wrongly figure that they've tried Jesus and he didn't work.

A Teacher's Power

Even though parents and teachers can't "get kids saved," we still have a huge role in bringing them to faith—but only if we work in step with the Spirit. We must use *his* formula. We must do what heralds ought to do with good news: tell it! God's method is that unbelievers "hear the word of the gospel and believe" (Acts 15:7).

Paul expressed the hope of such a teacher when he wrote to the Thessalonians: "God chose you as the firstfruits to be saved, through sanctification by the Spirit and belief in the truth. To this he called you through our gospel, so that you may obtain the glory of our Lord Jesus Christ" (2 Thessalonians 2:13–14). This passage says *God* chose the believers and *God* is the one making them holy. That's the Spirit's work. Yet it was Paul who actually spoke the good news. He even calls it *his* gospel. Paul had a powerful role in the Spirit's work because he spoke the good news, God's instrument to reach the lost. "Faith comes from hearing" (Romans 10:17).

No how-to-live lesson can wake the spiritually dead. You might as well be teaching corpses. If a kid is still dead in self-love, such a lesson will, at best, only get him to work harder at a selfish, manipulative sort of religion. But new life springs up where the good news is proclaimed. It hatches loving wonder at Jesus and true gratitude to God. "For it is the power of God for salvation to everyone who believes" (Romans 1:16).

You Get What You're Looking For

I once taught a teenaged boy who had not been baptized and wanted to be. This process required an interview with the elders. Over the years I've had the privilege of sitting in on a handful of such interviews with my students. This one, however, didn't go as smoothly as most.

The elder in charge asked the boy how he was saved. The boy answered that Jesus had died for him. Great answer, but it wasn't what the elder was looking for. "Yes, but how did *you* personally get saved?"

The boy was confused. "Well, Jesus took my sin when he died for me," he said. It took several minutes of prodding to finally get the boy to say he had accepted Jesus as his Savior, though he couldn't give details of the precise moment. The exhausted elder decided that would have to be good enough.

The elder was right to listen for a profession of faith, but what if he had followed up his first question by asking, "How do you know Jesus is at work in you?" I knew this kid. He could have given fantastic answers. His parents could have attested to them as well. He had a new attitude. He was trusting Jesus and eager to live for God. The elder, by looking for an *external decision* instead of *internal faith and repentance*, missed hearing a testimony that would have knocked his socks off.

We must set our eyes on the whole-person change authored by God and gladly embraced by a new Christian. This in no way lessens a kid's responsibility to respond in repentance and faith to the good news. There's nothing more fundamental for any of us to do our entire life: "This is the work of God, that you believe in him whom he has sent" (John 6:29). But kids will always choose according to their nature, and the conversion from a sinful nature to a reborn-by-the-Spirit one seldom comes by pressing for an external decision. It comes from being convicted of sin, hearing of God's saving love, and finding delight in the matchless person of Jesus.

Another Kind of Church Kid: Saved But Insecure

What about when kids become saved and start trying to live the Christian life? Well, that too must be in tandem with the Spirit, using the good news. Paul called it "the word of [God's] grace, which is able to build you up and to give you the inheritance among all those who are sanctified" (Acts 20:32). Saved kids need to see Jesus, too, so they can grow.

Many believers—especially young ones—don't have the good news so solidly planted in their souls that their Christian lives are joyful and filled with love. To identify what their faith is actually like, I assign them three descriptive names:

Anxious Alice

Alice doesn't have a deep sense of her total forgiveness and acceptance in Christ. She says she trusts Jesus, but she actually bases her sense of God's love for her on how well she manages to obey at the moment. She's constantly insecure, and her sins nag at her. She's convinced God is often disappointed with her and might not be saving her. Anxious Alice is *not able* to love God. How could she? She harbors a suspicion that he may actually be bent on sending her to hell, or at least is often annoyed with her. Since she's trying to impress God, she comes to resent him. When she says she loves him, she's only faking it—and she knows it.

Smug Sarah

Sarah doesn't have a deep sense of her sinfulness, so she's presumptuous and ungrateful. Even if she admits that she sometimes sins, she's convinced herself that she's not that bad—and she keeps up a good image to convince others as well. Smug Sarah, too, is *not able* to love God. She has no reason to. She's never come to grips with how much she mocks God and how much Jesus has done for her in spite of that. Besides, since she hardly sees her sin, she hardly feels any need to repent. She's not becoming a stronger Christian because she won't admit that she needs to.

Complacent Kyle

Kyle doesn't sense the full scope of the salvation God gives him. He doesn't see how Christ in him is the power of God to conquer sin and change him in thrilling ways. Now and then he may try to use his Christianity to become a better person, but he's not interested in fostering an all-out reliance on God that produces genuine holiness.

Complacent Kyle, like the others, is *not able* to love God. Why would he, when there's no thrill in the relationship? He may try to concoct some excitement by finding a ministry with a snazzy praise band and a fun leader, or by joining in some church project, but he's actually bored with Jesus.

Now, here's the kicker: many church kids I know struggle with all three of these at the same time. When I show these sketches to Christian teens and ask which they're most like, very few try to say none. Most have a hard time picking just one.

It seems puzzling that a kid can be both smug and anxious, but that's the sort of confusion that results when the good news isn't at the top of our minds. Only the good news fights both smugness and insecurity, declaring both that we're horribly sinful yet more loved by God than we could dare imagine. It also tells us that through the power of God working in us, we *can* change.

A Double Force

We make a mistake if we think kids are saved by hearing the good news and trusting Jesus, but then grow as Christians some other way. Paul tells the Colossians to continue in the faith they first had, "not shifting from the hope of the gospel that you heard" (Colossians 1:23). He underscores this a few verses later: "Therefore, as you received Christ Jesus the Lord, so walk in him, rooted and built up in him and established in the faith" (Colossians 2:6–7). We grow in the same way we became Christians—rooted in Jesus, with our hope in the good news.

Over the centuries, many believers have tried other ways to become more holy. Some have imposed rigid rules. Others have tried monk-like simplicity. Some have chased after mysterious blessings or secret religious rites. It's all in vain. They miss the simple word of the Bible.

The seventeenth-century English pastor Walter Marshall brilliantly pointed out that the good news is a double force in a believer's life.

- The good news that we're forgiven, adopted, and forever loved by God creates thankfulness and hope of life with Jesus. This *draws us* to him in love—like the tide pulls a ship.
- The good news that we're in Christ and given the Spirit means that we can rely on God's power in us. This is the *power* to flee from sin—like the wind propels that same ship.[3]

Tide *and* wind. Attraction *and* power. Pull *and* push. The good news is the double force believing kids need.

The First to Hear Good News

I learned more about this one summer at Bible camp. I was there to teach for a week from the Gospel of Luke. I decided my first lesson would come from Luke 2, where the real action starts with the birth of Jesus. Besides, that's where Luke introduces the *euangélion* in dramatic fashion, with the angel's announcement to the shepherds. What a great point I could make about how the good news came first to such lowly people!

To prep the lesson, I decided I at least ought to read through chapter 1 for context. It starts with an account of the priest Zechariah. There's high praise for his lifestyle. Zechariah was "righteous before God, walking blamelessly in all the commandments and statutes of the Lord" (Luke 1:6). He was chosen to offer incense in the temple, a rare and exciting duty.

In the middle of Zechariah's big moment, an angel appeared to tell him that his wife would give birth to a son as a prelude to God's Messiah. This was the joyful end to centuries of waiting. But Zechariah was more cautious than thrilled. He asked for a sign of confirmation. The angel was not pleased: "I am Gabriel. I stand in the presence of God, and I was sent to speak to you and to bring you this good news. And behold, you will be silent and unable to speak until the day that these things take place, because you did not believe my words" (Luke 1:19–20).

Wait. Good news? I read it again. I checked a Greek text. Sure enough, Gabriel said he was bringing *euangélion*.

The announcement to the shepherds wasn't the spot where Luke introduced the good news after all. Zechariah came first. The premise for my lesson was blown. More importantly, I had to see that Zechariah's righteous lifestyle mattered little once he showed his unbelief. He left the temple mute, using motions to try to explain what had happened, with limited success.

I needed to learn that Luke isn't just telling us that the good news arrived. He's showing us that believing it with joy is the defining dynamic of life—even for an upright church guy. These kids I was teaching weren't like the shepherds. They were kids whose parents shelled out money for Bible camp instead of, say, soccer camp or horseback-riding camp. They could quote Scripture. They knew how to behave inside a church building. *They were little Zechariahs.* They needed to hear that the good news came to a churchy guy. They needed to see how it had to become the centerpiece of his life with God.

Gabriel's announcement eventually did drill through to Zechariah's heart. When his son was born, he finally expressed his belief. Filled with the Spirit, he broke into song about God's saving kindness. It's not the sort of behavior you'd expect from such a proper, careful guy. But he was changed. He was overflowing with worship. His life with God was bigger than it'd been before, and better than his guarded approach in the temple.

Where Zechariah ended up is where we want our churchiest kids to end up. The path to that spot in the heart runs through the good news.

INSTRUCTIONS TO A TEACHER

Titus is a superb book for us to learn from because Paul wrote it to a teacher in the church. Over the course of one long sentence, he gives the reason believers obey God. As you read it, I'd like you to try to separate out the good news (what God does for us) from the good behavior (what we do for God).

For the grace of God has appeared, bringing salvation for all people, training us to renounce ungodliness and worldly passions, and to live self-controlled, upright, and godly lives in the present age, waiting for our blessed hope, the appearing of the glory of our great God and Savior Jesus Christ, who gave himself for us to redeem us from all lawlessness and to purify for himself a people for his own possession who are zealous for good works. (Titus 2:11–14)

How did you do? Not so well, I expect. The good news and godly living are so intertwined that it's hard to pick them apart! God's grace trains us to renounce ungodliness. The hope of Christ's return fuels our upright lives. Jesus gave himself to make us zealous for good works.

"Zealous." What a word! I recently helped a group of kids make a poster about the Ten Commandments with pictures of kids obeying. We wrote this passage from Titus on that poster to emphasize that we don't obey God grudgingly, or even just willingly. Because of the good news, we do it *zealously*. That's one of the purposes Jesus had in mind when he went to the cross.

If kids are leaving the church, it's because we've failed to give them a view of Jesus and his cross that's compelling enough to satisfy their spiritual hunger and give them the zeal they crave. They haven't seen that Jesus himself is better than any "Jesus program." He's better than the music used to worship him. He's better than a missions trip. He's better than their favorite youth leader. He's also better than money. Better than video games. Better than romantic teen movies. Better than sex. Better than popularity or power.

We've failed too many kids. We've fed them things to *do*. We've fed them "worshipful" experiences. But we've failed to feed them more than a spoonful of the good news. Now they're starving and they'll eat anything. They're trying to feed their souls with some*thing*—maybe even a churchy thing—that feels like it fits them, when what they need is some*one* utterly better than themselves.

Who Has the Best Answer?

Church kids don't just need the good news as much as other kids—they need it *more*. I saw an example of this while teaching at another Bible camp. Most of the campers were church kids, but not Ryan. His mom had signed him up because a neighbor had invited him and because camp was cheaper than other activities. Ryan had seldom been to church and didn't even have a Bible at home.

At the start of the week I wondered if Ryan would be able to keep up. I needn't have worried. He was my most attentive student, asking good questions and listening with excitement as I taught.

Most Bible teachers have experienced this phenomenon. Kids who are new to church are transfixed, while church kids hear the same lessons and remain ho-hum. Accepted wisdom says this is because the church kids have heard it before. But this time there was more to it. I was teaching the good news with every Bible story and the church kids were interested enough—they just weren't excited by it. I soon realized that they weren't even *noticing* the good news part of my teaching.

One evening near the end of the week I taught about King David and Mephibosheth. David had become king after his nemesis, Saul, died in battle. Not many descendants of Saul were left, which was good for David; they were a potential threat to his throne.

Mephibosheth was Saul's grandson. As a boy he'd been crippled, but survived and lived in an obscure home on the fringe of Israel's territory, away from his family's land. From David's perspective, this would have been a safe end for a potential enemy. But David was an extraordinary man who wanted to show kindness to a member of Saul's family, so he summoned Mephibosheth to the palace. The lame man must have been terrified, but David told him, "Do not fear, for . . . I will restore to you all the land of Saul your father, and you shall eat at my table always" (2 Samuel 9:7). David treated Mephibosheth like one of his own sons, and the Bible mentions three more times how Mephibosheth always ate at the king's table.

I asked the kids an open-ended question: "What can we learn about life with God from this lesson?"

Several hands shot up. "We should be kind too," said one. "God wants us to love our enemies," said another. More heads nodded in agreement. These were good answers. But were any of them the *best* answer?

"Anything else?" I asked. Nope. Everyone seemed to have the same thought.

Then I saw Ryan's hand. "It sounds like us and God," he said. "We're like Mephibosheth. We're the hurt guy who's not on God's side. But God is kind to us anyway. He's so good!"

Yup. That was the best answer, all right—and Ryan saw it before any of the church kids did. The church kids had years of experience with Bible lessons and had learned to respond to questions about God by thinking first, "What do I have to do for him now?" They'd need to *unlearn* this before they could admire Jesus as the King who invites them, his crippled enemies, to sit at his table. Both they and Ryan had heard the good news for a full week, but only Ryan was ready to respond to a question about God by thinking, "He's so good!"

How Christian Growth Stalls

There's one more reason kids who are raised in Christian homes and familiar with church need more of the good news. This time it isn't because of anything wrong; it's because *that's just how Christian growth works.*

As kids learn about God's goodness and holiness, they ought to increase in awe of him. That's growth. And as they examine themselves and see the ugliness inside, they ought to increase in conviction of sin. That's growth too. But the combination of these will drive them to despair—unless their understanding of the forgiveness and righteousness they have in Jesus also grows.

Think of a kid who's a new Christian as one starting to see God's light. As he learns, the beam of light in his life shows him two things: (1) God's holy demands and (2) the kid's sin in falling short of those demands. We at Serge use a helpful illustration of this.[4] The diagram shows these two things as the top edge and bottom edge of God's light. The kid also sees the cross, which covers the gap between the kid's sin and God's demands. The kid has joy and confidence. He's eager to live for God.

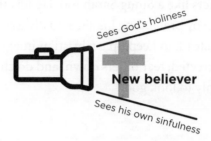

As his Christian life goes on, the kid learns more. His understanding of God's holy demands grows. He also sees more fully how neither his life nor his heart can ever measure up, so his understanding of his own sinfulness grows as well. The beam of light widens. And if he hasn't also been growing in appreciation for the good news—if the cross remains roughly the same size in his life—there will be gaps.

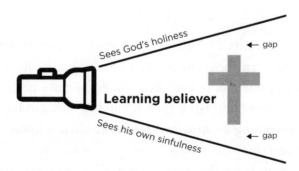

The kid becomes an Anxious Alice. He's aware that his good deeds aren't good enough and that his feelings for God aren't strong enough. He knows he's a hypocrite and is secretly haunted by guilt. He becomes a pretender, constantly scheming to make himself, his friends, and his parents believe the situation isn't so bad.

He tries working harder to do better, but with no success. So he also acts like a Complacent Kyle. He fills the gap between the cross and God's holiness by pretending that God's demands aren't really so extreme. Whatever little obedience he can muster up, he tells himself, must be okay.

The same kid acts like a Smug Sarah too. He fills the gap between the cross and his sin by pretending his sin actually isn't so horrible. He stops repenting. Instead, to keep up a Christian image, he will lie, get defensive when corrected, tear others down, and do churchy things or obey his parents only to look good.

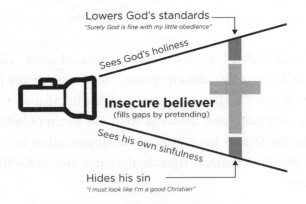

Lowers God's standards
"Surely God is fine with my little obedience"

Sees God's holiness

Insecure believer
(fills gaps by pretending)

Sees his own sinfulness

Hides his sin
"I must look like I'm a good Christian"

In short, the kid's Christian growth stalls. Learning more about God's greatness can't help him because he can't handle it. Telling him to sin less and obey more can't help either, because he fights back, tunes out, or does both. For a church kid, this stall can happen very soon after becoming a Christian because he already knows so much about God and sin.

The solution is for the cross to grow along with everything else. The more a kid learns about himself and God, the more he *must* learn to trust and delight in the good news too. He must become ever more certain that he's totally accepted in Christ, forgiven and adopted by God. It's the only way he can keep growing.

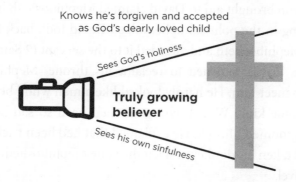

Knows he's forgiven and accepted
as God's dearly loved child

Sees God's holiness

**Truly growing
believer**

Sees his own sinfulness

The Bible tells us to expect this dynamic. Consider the prophet Isaiah, who had a thundering vision of God in the temple. His understanding of God's holiness grew huge in an instant, and he couldn't handle it: "Woe is me! For I am lost" (Isaiah 6:5). But an angel touched his lips with a hot coal and declared, "Your guilt is taken away, and your sin atoned for" (Isaiah 6:7). Only then, once Isaiah's bigger understanding of God's holiness and his own sin was matched by a bigger confidence in his forgiveness, was he ready for ministry.

A kid who's fed by the good news has a growing appreciation for Jesus and all he has done for him. That kid will be an amazing, nonpretending Christian. He won't try to look better than he is but instead will dare to confess sin openly and repent earnestly. He also won't have to pretend God is easily satisfied with a little churchy behavior, but he will dare to draw ever nearer to a holy God. This is because his sin and God's holiness just show him how much *more* he's been forgiven. They enlarge his love for Jesus.

LOVE FOR THE KING

The Mephibosheth account I shared above has one of my favorite endings of any story in the Bible. For years, Mephibosheth sat at David's table—a would-be enemy given the rights of a prince. But then David had to flee a revolt led by his son Absalom. All loyal members of David's court went with him.

Mephibosheth was not among the loyalists who left with David. A servant who brought aid to David claimed Mephibosheth hoped to be made king in the political upheaval, so David took back the land he'd given Mephibosheth and awarded it to the servant (2 Samuel 16).

In time, David returned to reclaim his throne. Mephibosheth came out to meet him. He hardly looked like a man who'd been plotting to become king. With David gone, he'd been so sad he hadn't washed or groomed himself. He explained that he'd been tricked. The servant had taken his donkey and left the lame Mephibosheth without a way to travel.

David was wishy-washy. He decided to have Mephibosheth and the opportunist servant split the land. But Mephibosheth's reply was perfect: "Oh, let him take it all, since my lord the king has come safely home" (2 Samuel 19:30).

That's the sort of devotion that comes from sitting daily at the table of our King, who has shown us such undeserved kindness. We are God's adopted children. When we remind ourselves of this good news every day, feasting on it, we come to care for the King himself rather than what he might give us. We come to love him.

QUESTIONS YOU MIGHT BE ASKING

The kids I teach already know the good news. We've been teaching about the cross and belief in Jesus since they were little. I can see the need for an occasional reminder, but isn't that enough?

This is a common way of thinking. We assume kids are well-grounded in the good news and that it's there in the background as we teach other stuff. But what's assumed is quickly forgotten. Without constant revival from the good news, kids—and adults—start trying to obey God under their own strength and willpower. The good news was never meant to be background. It's foreground—*the* source we look to for the power to do everything else. "Let us run with endurance the race that is set before us, *looking to Jesus*, the founder and perfecter of our faith" (Hebrews 12:1–2, emphasis mine).

But once they've heard the good news a certain number of times, what more of it could they possibly learn?

I learn more about the good news all the time. The older I get, the more I realize I've barely begun to understand the full richness of the person of Jesus and the blessings I have in him.

If your teaching of these things has become stale—and it happens with me too—I would encourage you to read and study the New Testament more. Look for what it says about Jesus and the blessings we share. It probably won't take long before you come across something you haven't thought much about. When you do, you'll have something new to say about the old good news. The "Gospel Transformation" series of small group studies from Serge—titled *Gospel Identity, Gospel Growth,* and *Gospel Love*—is also an excellent resource that can give you new insights into the blessings we have in Jesus.[5]

I sometimes use Paul's prayer for the Ephesians as a theme for my goal with kids: "that you, being rooted and grounded in love, may have strength to comprehend with all the saints what is the breadth and length and height and depth, and to know the love of Christ that surpasses knowledge, that you may be filled with all the fullness of God" (Ephesians 3:17–19). There's always room to go wider and deeper with the love of Christ—to learn more of it and have it sink further into our souls.

If conversion is a matter of God's work in a kid's heart, how do I tell which kids I teach are converted and which aren't?

Often, you can't tell for sure. The good thing is that since both need the same kind of teaching—large helpings of the good news and encouragement to believe it and repent—you don't have to figure it out. I seldom try.

Then do you treat kids as if they're already saved or as if they aren't?

Sometimes when I urge kids to believe, I'll acknowledge the difference. I'll tell them they may need to believe for the first time or they may need to believe more deeply to grow. But usually I talk to church kids as if they're already saved. If they're part of the church family we ought to prayerfully expect God to be working in them, even if we know it's possible they actually aren't converted.

For example, take Nicole, the girl I shared the God Report Card with in our last chapter. I spoke to her as if she were an insecure believer, but I knew very well that she might have not been converted and was just doing churchy things for some selfish reason. It didn't matter in terms of what I had to teach her; in either case, she had to hear the good news and believe it. That's the beauty of it.

Show Them Jesus Right Away

Pick something you'll do to put the ideas from this chapter to work. Here are some possibilities:

Anyone: Because becoming a Christian and growing in Christ is the *Spirit's* work, begin to pray regularly for God to work in the lives of the kids you teach. Add it to your personal prayers. Or if you struggle to keep up a personal prayer routine, add it to the regular prayers you say with your kids. Make it part of weekly classroom prayer, family devotions, or bedtime prayers. If you aren't sure whether or not the kids you're praying for are believers, you can pray something like "Father, work in _____'s heart to grow great faith and love for you." That's something both non-believers and believers need.

Parents: Do an honest self-assessment of what you're trusting to make you feel good about your kids' salvation. It might be

____ their good behavior.
____ your family's Christian heritage or church activities.
____ a prayer they said or a public decision they made.

These can be good things. But if your hope is in these things rather than in God—that he's working in your kids' hearts—confess this to God now. Ask your Father to be their Father too. Then set up a time with your spouse, or place a reminder where you'll see it daily, to pray every day for God to work in your kids' hearts. That consistent prayer is perhaps the single most hands-on thing you can add to your schedule—and *do*—to help your kids come to faith and grow in Christ.

Teachers: The next time you teach a lesson based on a Bible story, test your class by asking them how *they* would apply the story. Use the same open-ended question I asked at camp: "What can we learn about life with God from this story?" If your students have much to say about how they need to behave better but little to say about what God does, it's a safe bet they aren't used to hearing the good news. Tell them that learning how to behave is an excellent way to use the Bible, but often the very *best* thing is to notice and appreciate how *God* behaves. Keep asking the question, lesson after lesson, until they learn to look for God and find delight in him.

Youth workers: Show the young people you lead the sketches of the three kinds of church kids who aren't growing: Anxious Alice, Smug Sarah, and Complacent Kyle (changing the names if any of your kids happen to share them). Ask which sketch sounds most like their own Christian lives, and use that question to launch a discussion about how stronger belief in Jesus and his good news can help them grow. Do they need to more deeply believe their sinfulness? Their forgiveness in Christ? The power he gives to overcome their sin? Or maybe all three? Make sure the point of the discussion is to encourage kids to grow in their faith by first of all believing the good news more deeply.

Chapter 4
The Factory-Preset Fourth Grader

Because the good news changes hard hearts
Of the numerous changes in our character or deportment,
how many are deceitful, how few are real and deep!
Only that which can go down into the very depths of our spiritual
being can produce any change that is worthy of the name.
The one spell that can really transform us is THE CROSS.
—Horatius Bonar1

It had been a good Sunday morning with my group of fourth graders. They'd behaved, prayed with sincerity, and participated well as I taught a lesson about Abraham. Now it was snack time. The person in charge of such things had left us with one cheese stick for each kid and a package of crackers to divide between them.

Exactly thirty-four crackers. For nine kids. I knew because one of the kids, eager to make sure he got his fair share, counted them. It's amazing how sharp math skills become when snacks are served. Another kid did the division and announced that this meant four crackers each—except for two kids who'd have to settle for three.

"I get four!" one kid demanded.

"No," another said, "we need to split them." Some started arguing over how best to break up the extra crackers. Others were putting pressure on the timid kids to eat just three. Greed had taken over. It was so ingrained that it extended to fractions of a cracker.

I decided to put an end to it. "Everyone gets three crackers," I announced.

"What about the leftovers?" someone asked.

"They stay left over," I said. "Nobody eats them." Case settled. Except it wasn't, and I knew it. I'd stopped the argument but done nothing about the greed.

A Forgotten Lesson

We've all seen this sort of behavior, with all ages of kids—and adults. Toddlers in the nursery fight over a toy. High-school guys angle for the biggest slice of pizza.

But that morning with my fourth graders, as they settled down and started eating their cheese and crackers, I realized the argument I'd just witnessed should never have happened. Not on that particular day. You see, the lesson I'd just finished teaching—minutes before snack time—had been about how we can avoid being greedy. Yet greed was such a habit that the moment I brought out the crackers, they forgot the lesson.

Even worse, I had forgotten it too. I'd killed off the argument without referring back to the lesson at all. I'd stupidly missed an obvious opportunity to use the cracker incident to apply what I'd been teaching.

The particular part of Abraham's life we had studied was the account of when he and his nephew Lot separated in Canaan. God promised to bless Abraham and to give his offspring all the land, but Abraham had to learn to actually believe these promises. Early on he still operated under look-out-for-myself thinking. It led him to tell lies about his wife in Egypt.

His dispute with Lot over grazing land was his second crisis, and he responded better. Abraham suggested they divide the area, and he let Lot pick first. Lot chose selfishly. He grabbed the lush river valley, leaving Abraham the dry hill country.

We spent most of the lesson time discussing how Abraham could be so unselfish that he let Lot choose first. Abraham was the elder patriarch. Custom demanded he get the choice pick. I asked the kids how Abraham could give up such a valuable right when we fight over things as trivial as being first at the water fountain. They understood that Abraham must have believed God's promises. He'd learned that the best things in life come from God, unearned. Abraham could give up the best part of the land because he knew God was giving him a far bigger inheritance.

We talked about how this applies to us. We discussed how God gives us even bigger blessings than Abraham got, that we'll have a home with Jesus forever and share all his riches. The more we're gripped by this truth, the more we won't feel a need to be greedy for this life's lesser trinkets.

That was the lesson. I'd just taught *all* that. So as the kids munched down the last of those crackers, I decided to make up for missing the application earlier. I asked them, "What does today's lesson have to do with how you acted with the crackers?"

"Huh?"

"You were arguing over the crackers," I said. "Did you forget what today's lesson was about?"

Slowly, one boy made a connection. "We're supposed to not be greedy," he said. Another chimed in. "That's right. Don't be greedy. I guess we broke God's rules."

Other kids nodded in agreement. They felt scolded. "We forgot," they told me. "We'll do better next time. We'll try harder not to be greedy."

I just stood there. Could I have done *that* badly? That wasn't the lesson I'd taught at all!

THE HEART'S DEFAULT SETTING

I tell this story to show you where kids' hearts will naturally go, even when we teach well. I'd taught a good-news lesson. I'd carefully avoided moralizing, instead showing God's love and our blessings in Christ. I'd encouraged the kids to believe that good news above all. Even so, in their hearts they'd turned it into nothing but a what-you-must-do-for-God lesson.

This is the way everyone's heart naturally works. Our kids are programmed to try to earn points with God. Like a piece of electronics shipped from the factory with default settings, they're preset *not to believe* the good news. This trust in their religious and moral efforts takes the place of trusting Jesus. It's so strong that even when you teach a good-news lesson, they easily get the wrong idea.

I should point out that not all good-news lessons end in frustration. Many times I've seen the Spirit use the good news to break into kids' hearts. Still, the scheming drive to impress God by what we've done is deeply embedded in our corrupted programming. Removing it requires being intentional. It takes deliberately pounding home the good news, over and over again.

WHY LOVE ISN'T OPTIONAL

So there we are in front of the classroom. Or we're chatting with a youth group. Maybe we're having lunch with a struggling teenager, or driving our own kids to soccer practice. We know the kids we're with have changes they need to make in their Christian lives, but often we don't know what to say beyond "stop doing that" or "God wants you to do this."

At such a moment the issue is not *what* those kids should do—it's *how* to reach their hearts. They need to rest in Jesus until they have such joy over his beauty and what he's done for them that it spills out into the way they live. It sounds hokey, but our goal must be to build love for God. There are at least two reasons for this.

Christian behavior isn't real obedience unless it starts with love for God.

When Jesus was asked which commandment was most foundational, he said, "You shall love the Lord your God with all your heart and with all your soul and with all your mind. This is the great and first commandment" (Matthew 22:37–38). Anytime we settle for "obedience" without love, we aren't being serious about the most important obedience of all. Nothing and nobody may come ahead of Jesus. He used scandalously strong language to explain how far above any other loves our love for him must be: "If anyone comes to me and does not hate his own father and mother and wife and children and brothers and sisters, yes, and even his own life, he cannot be my disciple" (Luke 14:26).

There's no power to obey vigorously without love for Jesus.

Jesus also said, "Whoever has my commandments and keeps them, he it is who loves me" (John 14:21). That great and first commandment is the one the others hang on. Any time we don't keep one of the others, it's clear we didn't keep the first one. We loved ourselves more than Jesus.

We might convince some kids to be good churchgoers and to say their prayers and such at home even if they don't love God, but at best they'll just be working harder at a selfish, manipulative religion that God rejects. Joyless pretending is dangerous to kids. It looks like holy living and makes them think they're following Jesus—when, in fact, their hearts remain cold. We *must* go after the heart.

The Bible's answer to how love grows is the good news: "We love because he first loved us" (1 John 4:19). The good-news teacher skillfully steers a kid's heart by showing the breathtaking beauty of Jesus. Only Jesus can capture hearts that are bound to the approval of friends or the fun of video games. Only he is more worthy of their love.

Once kids grasp this, they won't merely admit, grudgingly, that they need to try harder—they'll look forward to it. When they're confronted with their greed over some crackers, or with any other sin, they won't say, "We broke God's rules." Their first thought will be, "We broke our Father's heart."

How I've Taught It Wrong

The prophets spoke of how God demands a pure heart above external obedience: "This people draw near with their mouth and honor me with their lips, while their hearts are far from me" (Isaiah 29:13). Jesus quoted that verse to the obedient-looking Pharisees. He also said the heart drives behavior: "The good person out of the good treasure of his heart produces good, and the evil person out of his evil treasure produces evil, for out of the abundance of the heart his mouth speaks" (Luke 6:45).

Even though I know this, I too often ignore the heart in my own teaching. It seems too much to expect hearts to change, so I go for what's easy. I fall back on lesser motivations that are proven to bring short-term, external results. After all, I can *get* a fourth grader to take just three crackers. And because I'm good at persuasion, I might even convince a teenager to do something big—like stop lying to his parents or put off having sex. I can stop the evil act—for a while. So I choose to do *that*, instead of deal with the evil heart from which those acts come.

These are some of the motivations I've used over the years. Perhaps some of them will be familiar to you as well.

I've appealed to pride.

I've told kids that if they obey God, they can feel good about themselves because they're being good Christians. They can hold their head high knowing they're pleasing Jesus, their parents, and me.

I've appealed to self-interest.

I've told kids that following God's rules is the only way they can be happy and satisfied in life. God knows best, and they should live his way if they want things to work out.

I've appealed to fear and reward.

I've suggested that God will punish bad deeds and dole out blessings for good ones. Kids can't expect their prayers to be answered if they're living in disobedience, after all.

I've even resorted to blissful blindness.

I've grown tired of saying "do better," so I've given kids comforting talks about God's love without seriously addressing their sin. Perhaps I've even tossed in a few feel-good, high-energy activities. The kids go away feeling happy about God—because they had fun. Maybe that'll help.

Some of these arguments are true, especially the one about how obeying God is good for you. But at best, they're secondary motivations. At worst, they're all about self. Self-esteem. Self-preservation. Self-advancement. Selfishness dressed up to look Christian. I ought to hate it when I talk kids into such selfish repentance! And I shouldn't be surprised when it doesn't last.

A few years ago youth leaders were shocked by a study that showed teens who took a pledge to refrain from sex until marriage ended up no more likely to put off sex than kids from similar backgrounds who didn't take the pledge.[2] These kids had determined to please God and their parents. They'd been told again and again how chastity would make them happier in the long run. They'd been honored in ceremonies designed to give them pride in their decision. But it was all self-based. None of it got to their hearts.

WE BELIEVE IN REAL CHANGE

Unbelievers always think selfish reasons like these are why Christians behave. They have no hope that hearts can actually change. But those worldly approaches ought to be dead in us. We believe in lasting, Spirit-fed renewal. When we motivate kids with the good news, we reject the nonsense that they just need to make a few life adjustments as they create a spiritual journey. The good news tells the truth—that kids *need to be crucifying sin in their lives*. They are prone to horrendous acts of rebellion against a jealous God, and he does not take it lightly. Sin is deadly serious.

Jesus takes sin most seriously of all. He's the guy who said to cut off your hand if it makes you sin. But to understand how serious Jesus is about sin, consider also how he left heaven to live as one of us in his world we've messed up. He got hungry and tired. People misunderstood him. He was beaten, laughed at, and spat on. He let himself be nailed to a cross and killed there, bearing the curse for our adultery, to set us free. Our sins are all paid for—not just the few sins we notice but the whole ugly heart that secretly loves them. All forgiven.

The good news takes us daily from despair to astonished laughter. With relief in our eyes we look at the man who's done all this for us. And who do we see? We see the strongest yet gentlest, most regal and yet most humble person imaginable. Most of all, we see the kind of lover we've never known before. Jesus's love for us is pure love. It has nothing to do with us being the least bit lovely. If it did, we'd feel pressure to keep up whatever earned his love. But no, "if we are faithless, he remains faithful" (2 Timothy 2:13). He loves us forever. No payback needed. No conditions. No guilt trips. We are loved, period.

And where *that* is believed, the heart is won.

TEACHER'S JOB, STUDENTS' JOB

Several years ago, when I was first starting to change my teaching, I taught at a weekend youth retreat. At the start of the weekend I asked those church kids what they expected from me and what I should expect from them. They told me my job was to tell them what God says to do in the Bible. Their job was to listen well and then do it. Some of them surely had other reasons as well for being at the retreat, but mostly they were serious. They wanted to study and grow.

It was just the answer I expected. I had set them up.

My teaching that weekend was a series of lessons from the life of the disciple Simon Peter. The first passage we looked at was where Jesus helped him catch a boatload of fish. Peter was already acquainted with Jesus, so it's not surprising that Jesus was teaching from Peter's fishing boat. Luke tells the story.

> And when he had finished speaking, he said to Simon, "Put out into the deep and let down your nets for a catch." And Simon answered, "Master, we toiled all night and took nothing! But at your word I will let down the nets." And when they had done this, they enclosed a large number of fish, and their nets were breaking. They signaled to their partners in the other boat to come and help them. And they came and filled both the boats, so that they began to sink. But when Simon Peter saw it, he fell down at Jesus' knees, saying, "Depart from me, for I am a sinful man, O Lord." For he and all who were with him were astonished at the catch of fish that they had taken, and so also were James and John, sons of Zebedee, who were partners with Simon. And Jesus said to Simon, "Do not be afraid; from now on you will be catching men." And when they had brought their boats to land, they left everything and followed him (Luke 5:4–11).

After reading through the passage, I took the students back to where Jesus first told Peter to go fishing. I said, "Look at Peter's response—'We toiled all night and took nothing! But at your word I will let down the nets.' What do you think of that? Is that a good response to Jesus?"

I expected a lively debate, but I didn't get one. Instead, an older girl started talking about how Peter obeyed despite his misgivings. She was highly impressed. That's the hardest kind of obedience, she explained, and Peter deserved much praise for putting down those nets. "That's the way we all need to be," she said. "We need to obey Jesus even when it's hard. What Peter did was the best!"

There were grunts of approval all around. No one seemed to disagree.

I challenged her, "But if you look at the whole story, doesn't it seem like Peter became an even stronger follower *after* that?" I asked. "Don't you think Peter grows in this story?" No, she didn't.

"What about when he falls down in worship of Jesus?" I asked. She'd noticed that, but it didn't seem as impressive as putting down the nets.

I understood. That girl knew all about trying to do what Jesus says. But she knew hardly anything about meeting Jesus himself as a person—or being awed by him. The concept barely registered.

How Peter Grew

At this point, you too may be thinking Peter did well to put down those nets. Okay, I agree it was admirable. Peter already had *some* faith. But I beg you to see also that as we come to know Jesus better, life with him gets better too.

Before he caught all those fish, Peter was hesitant but willing; afterward, he was eager. Before, Peter figured the report of a seasoned fisherman ought to count for something; afterward, he found himself unworthy to do anything but fall at Jesus's knees. Before, Peter could crow about how he put down those nets despite how foolish it sounded—notice how he announced his obedience! Afterward, the silly idea that he had to help Jesus was erased by how Jesus helped him.

And before, Peter's focus was misplaced. Think about it. He was in a boat with the eternal Son of God, and his mind was on *fish*. Afterward, he adored Jesus as infinitely beyond anything else that had once been important in his life. The story isn't about Peter being a hero; it's about him finding a Hero who captures his heart.

Peter also saw who he was when joined to Jesus. He asked Jesus to go away—which is sensible once you've realized that you're a selfish sinner sitting next to God. But Jesus didn't go away. Jesus never leaves those who know they're sinners and trust him. Instead, he called Peter to join in the work of catching men.

Peter had just learned he didn't deserve to share a boat with Jesus, much less work with him. Just the opportunity to go with Jesus was pure grace. There would be no more trying to impress. It wouldn't be one of those jobs with a dreaded quarterly performance review that might get him fired. If performance were the issue, he wouldn't have been called in the first place.

What an improbable thrill to be joined to Jesus! "*Who, me?*" No wonder Peter eagerly left everything—boats, family, all those fish. His devotion to Jesus hit a new level, and it wasn't because he had learned a new way to obey and determined to do it. It was because of his experience of Jesus himself.

How We Can Grow Too

We too are sinners loved by a holy God, saved through the surprising blood of the one and only Jesus. And we too are called by grace, set free from anxiety and commissioned to do good works. That's what I wanted those kids to experience on the retreat. I ended the lesson by telling them that their idea about my job and theirs was partly right. I too wanted them to obey better, but it wouldn't come by studying good behavior—it would come by studying and receiving the good news. Through Peter's eyes we would try to catch some of the wonder he knew in Jesus. It would become our fuel.

SPIRITUAL KING-OF-THE-HILL

Now, many years later, I sometimes use an illustration to show kids how this works. It's based on the game king-of-the-hill. You know the one—a kid stands on a mound and the others try to push him off and take his place. The biggest and toughest kid usually spends the most time being king.

We often imagine the Christian life is like a game of king-of-the-hill played between our heart and our head. On the hill is the heart with the sins we still love to do. Trying to push it off is the head with the godly things we know we *should* do. Such is the Christian life, we think—a constant battle between head and heart.

Which will win this shoving match? Well, the head might be on top now and then. But in most people the heart wins most of the time. "But what comes out of the mouth proceeds from the heart" (Matthew 15:18).

What's the solution, then? We must bring in a bigger heart to battle the sin we love. Only a stronger love for Jesus can overpower and displace our love of sin.

John wrote, "If anyone loves the world, the love of the Father is not in him" (1 John 2:15). Jesus taught, "No one can serve two masters, for either he will hate the one and love the other, or he will be devoted to the one and despise the other" (Matthew 6:24). Both tell us that we can't love sin and love God at the same time. One love pushes out the other.[3]

Two Kinds of Kids

A kid who builds love for God by believing the good news ends up living differently than a kid who's trying to please God through good behavior. A good-behavior kid is still seeking love and approval. A good-news kid knows he's already loved forever by his heavenly Father, and actually behaves better.

A good-behavior kid...	**A good-news kid...**
Divides the world into good people and bad people. Like Peter before he caught the fish, constantly tries to prove himself to be one of the good kids.	Sees only bad people and one good person—Jesus. Like Peter after he caught the fish, spends his life trusting and following that one good guy.
Is prone to sins of the tongue. Tells lies to protect her image, gets defensive when others criticize her, and gossips to make herself look better than others.	Admits when she's wrong and allows others to correct her without fear because her confidence is in Christ. Tells others about her weaknesses and congratulates them for their strengths.
Mostly points out how others do wrong. Often talks about himself in comparison to others—like the Pharisee at the temple in Jesus's parable: "God, I thank you that I am not like other men" (Luke 18:11).	Lets the sins of others go unnoticed. Knows God loves him whatever he's done, so willingly confesses his own sins—like the tax collector in Jesus's parable: "God, be merciful to me, a sinner!" (Luke 18:13).
Participates in worship, prayer, and Bible study so that God or others will see and approve. Is conscious of what others think when praying aloud or speaking up in a group.	Participates in worship, prayer, and Bible study because she loves God and fellowship with him is a joy.
Needs for parents, teachers, and other kids to notice when she's been good. May obey at home and church but struggle with behavior at school or with non-Christian friends—when no believers are watching.	Obeys God even when no one else is around to notice it. Doesn't need to be rewarded with praise because, joined to Jesus, she feels enough approval from God already.
Only participates reluctantly in "embarrassing" Christian activities like telling others about Jesus. Is torn between what people outside the church will think and what those inside think, and is troubled with guilt over what God thinks.	Doesn't worry what others think because he knows God loves him as a child. Jesus's love for him makes him eager to tell others.
May prefer light, "fun" church activities to those that involve real worship, serious study, or meaningful confession of sin. Those latter things carry too much pressure or self-exposure to be comfortable.	Enjoys having fun with other believers, but mostly because the joy and freedom she feels in Christ spills over. Worship, Bible study, and confession of sin fuel her relationship with God—and with other believers.

Look at that list again. You might think the good-news ideal is so far from your actual experience with kids that it isn't realistic. But it's what God calls them to be, and it's a blessing he promises—so we must build kids up to it. Week after week, year after year, we must give them a foundation in the good news.

How Peter Grew . . . More

The youth retreat ended up building some of that foundation. Those kids and I worked hard, studying the Bible to see Jesus and be amazed.

Along with Peter, we watched as Jesus took a twelve-year-old girl's hand and brought her back to life, giving orders not to tell anyone about it even though the crowd outside had been laughing at him. Amazing. We watched Jesus challenge his disciples to feed five thousand people with a boy's lunch—and when they claimed it was impossible, show them it wasn't. We watched him send those guys out in a boat to be rocked by a storm, come to them walking on the water, call Peter to join him, and quiet the storm in an instant—an unforgettable lesson on the power of faith. More amazing.

To close out the retreat, we looked at Peter three years after the incident with the fish. *Three years with Jesus.* Yet on the night before Jesus died, Peter still had more to see of him. Peter's betrayal that night was a staggering failure. Jesus gave him the honor of preparing the Passover meal, sacrificing and cooking a lamb. Then during the meal, Jesus warned Peter he'd get scared and deny him. Peter couldn't imagine such a thing. His bluster got the better of him: "Even if I must die with you, I will not deny you!" (Matthew 26:35). And he meant it.

But after Jesus was arrested, members of the gang that grabbed him thought they recognized Peter—and Peter denied being Jesus's friend. Three times. To be extra-convincing, he punctuated the last denial with a curse. Tears followed, and much shame. At first, Peter couldn't see what had really happened.

Jesus had gone to the cross to save sinners—sinners like Peter. While Peter was saving his own skin by denying Jesus, Jesus was saving Peter by taking the punishment for that disloyalty. He wasn't just the Holy One who stooped to share a boat with Peter. He was the perfect Son of God who suffered and died for Peter—that was the most amazing thing of all.

It's why years later Peter could remember that night—the one with the lamb and the cross—and write, "You were ransomed from the futile ways inherited from your forefathers, not with perishable things such as silver or gold, but with the precious blood of Christ, like that of a lamb without blemish or spot" (1 Peter 1:18–19). Peter became a bold leader in the church. He knew he was safe in Jesus, who loved him through and through.

THE WORLD'S BEST JOB

Like Peter, those kids and I expanded our grasp of the good news that weekend. I feel sure it helped some of them. I know it helped me. I still remember how studying the Gospels with the central purpose of better knowing Jesus and his love for me was *exciting*. It killed off the need to impress God and put in its place a far more powerful incentive to obey—the duties that come with love.

That's why the good news beats good behavior. And it's why I've never looked back to my old methods.

Maybe you've felt frustrated as a teacher or parent. You've taught kids how to live for God. You've applied your best persuasion. But they keep living for themselves, and you aren't sure what to do. Don't be discouraged. Kids will need correction sometimes, but our mission is not to hound or plead or talk them into anything—it's to speak God's word of salvation, peace, faith, and the righteousness Christ gives. These are the things Paul calls "the whole armor of God, that you may be able to stand against the schemes of the devil" (Ephesians 6:11).

Nothing could make kids more ready for the battles they will face in life. Nothing could better equip them to be obedient and safe from temptation. I can't imagine a better ministry.

Questions You Might Be Asking

I understand you want kids to grow by studying the good news, not good behavior. Are you saying it's bad to study good behavior? That doesn't seem right.

It's good and necessary to study God's commands and to work hard to obey them. One of their functions is to show us how to live—and what it looks like when love for God and others shapes all we do. However, this becomes a problem if it gets to be pretty much the only reason you open the Bible. This is because another function of those commands (and of the whole Bible) is to show us our sin and drive us to believe in Jesus.

When we focus on good behavior, we end up with kids who worry about impressing God and for whom the good news is an afterthought. That's why I focus on the good news. Please don't take it to mean there's no place for studying how we should behave. A kid whose heart is touched by the good news will come to love studying God's commands because they teach him how to be like Christ. Those commands will become both a blessing to him and something he works at. Don't imagine he'll see God's love and—poof!—sin will no longer be a problem; obeying still takes effort and study. We just need to be sure that such a kid remains constantly grounded in the good news, because it's foundational.

You set the bar awfully high when you say kids aren't fully obeying unless they love God and enjoy him. Is that realistic?

I set the bar where Jesus set it. And it's *his* work in us that makes it happen. To say love and joy are too high a goal is to say we don't expect much from God. We all sin and fall way short of this demand, of course. But as kids take hold of the good news and continually enjoy forgiveness, there will be progress and a growing love for God. The first two qualities listed for the fruit of the Spirit are love and joy (Galatians 5:22). If kids have "obedience" without love and joy we have to wonder if it comes from the Spirit at all.

So does that mean that instead of telling kids to be good in other ways I should first tell them to love God?

No, it means you should first tell them the good news and urge them to believe it. None of us learns to love anyone—including God— by having someone *tell* us to love them. You love people because you find them beautiful and lovable, and because they love you. The good thing is that God is far, far more beautiful and love-worthy than anything or anyone else, and he loves us far, far more than anyone else ever could. As kids learn this good news and believe it, love for God will naturally follow. That's why Jesus can insist on love for God as the highest command. God deserves such love, and failure to see it is a travesty.

You say God loves us, period, without us being at all lovely. Are you sure God doesn't see anything *lovely in us?*

God's eternal love for his children is unchanging and has nothing to do with us being worthy of his love: "God shows his love for us in that while we were still sinners, Christ died for us" (Romans 5:8). We can't change God. We don't make his love stronger or weaker by anything we do. This unique, perfect love is what gives us security, confidence, and gratitude. "Perfect love casts out fear" (1 John 4:18).

But God's love has many sides, so there's a sense in which he also loves us for who we've become in Christ. Joined to Jesus, we do lovely things. In this sense we *can* say that God does love us for how we're lovely. It's why Jesus could say, "He who loves me will be loved by my Father" (John 14:21). However, this shouldn't make us think we earn God's love, or that this is the basis for his acceptance of us. It only makes us more certain that God loves us utterly, in every way, far beyond what we deserve.

Doesn't the Bible use our self-interest to motivate us to obey God? Why are you so set against it?

Life in Christ is full of blessings. So serving God *is* in our self-interest, and the Bible often points this out. It mentions things like avoiding judgment and having a happier life. These are all sensible reasons to obey God. But to serve God *only* out of self-interest is to miss the core of who God is. God himself is self-giving and full of love—just look at the cross. We can hardly say we're God's people if we live only out of self-interest. It's good to point out all the benefits of obeying God so long as the power of the good news to transform hearts isn't lost in the process. The Bible gives us many motivations, all valid, but the top one is love for a God who has loved us.

But don't we often need to be more forceful in urging kids to obey, using tough tactics like threats of God's punishment?

Warnings about disobedience are all through the Bible. We must take them seriously, and be glad for God's fatherly discipline that corrects us when we're stuck in sin. That said, it's a mistake to think that a threatening approach is more forceful than the good news. A teacher who focuses on the Bible's threats and rewards has to be very careful not to push too hard, because kids easily end up either in despair (if they fail to obey) or proud (if they do obey). It's better when kids are strongly grounded in the good news—secure in knowing God loves them, *period*. Then a teacher can actually dare to be much more forceful about urging them to obey God.

SHOW THEM JESUS RIGHT AWAY

Start taking a heart-centered approach with your kids now. Consider picking one of these ideas and doing it:

Parents: Use the "armor of God" to bless and pray for your kids. Follow these steps:

1. Prepare six index cards by writing one piece of the good-news "armor" from Ephesians 6:14–17 on each card. The pieces are truth, righteousness, peace, faith, salvation, and the word of God. If you like, decorate the cards by including a picture of the belt, breastplate, etc., that goes with each piece.

2. Every few days at mealtime or bedtime, let your child pick out a card. Then encourage your child by telling her something Jesus has done for her that's related to that armor piece. The following are examples:

- *Truth*: "You can be sure that everything Jesus says is true and good for you."
- *Righteousness*: "Only Jesus gives you the perfect righteousness you can't earn."
- *Peace*: "Jesus has made peace with God by dying for your sins."
- *Faith*: "Faith in Jesus will never fail you. There's nothing better to put your faith in."
- *Salvation*: "Jesus saves you from every evil caused by sin."
- *Word of God*: "No power on earth is a match for the powerful word of Jesus."

3. Then follow the instruction of Ephesians 6:18 and pray with your child that believing this good news will strengthen her to fight sin in her life.

Teachers: Use the illustration of the heart-vs.-head, king-of-the-hill game with your students. Draw a head and write "Good Things I Know I *Should* Do" on it. On another sheet of paper, draw a heart and write "Bad Things I Still Love to Do" on it. Ask your class which usually wins out in their lives. (I've found that even young kids, if they're honest, understand that the heart usually wins.) Finally, show them a bigger heart with "Love for Jesus" written on it. Discuss how we need to pursue more love for Jesus if we want to displace love for sin, and how we might start doing that.

Youth leaders: Copy the list of differences between a good-behavior kid and a good-news kid from this chapter, and use it as a starting point for discussion. Ask your group questions like the following: Which of these best describes you? Why don't you act more like someone who firmly believes the good news of Jesus? How would your life change if you *did* believe the good news more deeply? What do you think we might do as a group to help each other have deeper faith in what Jesus gives us? What might you do personally to nurture deeper belief in Jesus?

Chapter 5

The Mom in Queen Esther's Bedroom

Because the good news is the Bible's theme song

Christ alone makes all other things suddenly vanish.
—John Calvin1

I saw her lurking outside my classroom—the mom of one of my students. I was a few minutes into teaching a Bible lesson, and I noticed her through the window of the classroom door. No big deal. Parents come by all the time, and I figured she needed to pick up her kid. She seemed hesitant to interrupt the class, so I motioned for her to come on in.

She opened the door. "I'm sorry, would it be okay for me to sit in?" she asked.

"Of course," I told her. I had a standing invitation for any parent to visit any class, and I was always happy when one took me up on it. Mom took a seat among the kids, and I turned back to my lesson. "Let's see, where was I?"

"Oh. This might be a problem," I thought to myself.

ESTHER IN PICTURES

That day I was teaching older elementary kids from the book of Esther. It's a first-rate tale for a guy like me who likes telling stories. I'd been using a large whiteboard and colored markers to recreate the setting—the capital city in Persia—with stick figures for the characters.

Before class I'd drawn all the locations—city streets; the palace gate; the king's throne room, banquet hall, and bed chamber; the queen's palace and banquet hall; the chief nobleman's residence; a treasury building; housing for the king's harem. And gallows—not the hangman's sort we know but period-authentic poles with spikes at the top for impaling and displaying the bodies of the king's enemies.

The story starts with King Xerxes looking for a new queen after the old one proved too headstrong. The prettiest girls in the land were brought into his harem and given a year of training. Each then had a turn with him for one night. Afterwards, they moved into a second harem for girls the king was done with, never to see him again unless he asked. The one he liked best would become the new queen. Yuck.

Esther was the Persian name of a young Jewish woman living in the city with her cousin Mordecai. That right there makes us wonder about her. She wasn't among the more devout Jews who moved back to Jerusalem when the nation's exile ended. Had her family given in to Persia's charms? Had she forgotten she was one of God's chosen people—called to be different?

Well, Esther got conscripted into the king's harem. It was hardly a place for a nice girl, but she thrived. She listened well and learned how to please the king. After her night with him, he picked her for his queen. Meanwhile, Mordecai sat at the king's gate and uncovered an assassination plot. He reported two traitors, whom the king hung on the gallows.

At this point in the story I'd taken markers to my whiteboard scene and added stick figures for the traitors impaled at the top of the gallows. The kids loved this.

"Put some blood," one kid urged me. "You need to make them bloody."

I wasn't so sure. The bodies on the gallows were gruesome enough. I was pushing the boundaries of good taste. But the kids kept begging and I gave in. I added red smears to those bodies in my picture and got back to telling the story.

That was when I noticed Mom outside the classroom.

SEX, VIOLENCE, AND JESUS

Before you think I'm reckless, I should mention that I'd carefully considered whether or not to include both the traitors and the process for choosing a queen in my lesson. I'd even tried prepping a lesson without the sex and violence. I thought of ways to gloss over the unpleasant stuff and just present Esther as a young woman admired for her bravery. But sanitizing the Bible that way had left me without anything meaningful to say about God or to celebrate in Jesus, so I chose the unedited approach, which was more faithful to the Bible anyway. I was now second-guessing myself, but I pressed on. I had a reason for drawing harems and speared guys on poles, and I needed to get to it.

In the Bible story, Mordecai proved faithful to God. He refused to bow before the king's chief nobleman, Haman, whose family were enemies of God's people. Feeling dishonored, Haman erected an extra-tall gallows and planned to hang Mordecai on it. He also made a donation to the king's treasury, sneakily winning permission to kill all Jews in the empire.

Only Esther might be positioned to stop the slaughter. However, to approach the king and ask would violate the palace rules she'd mastered. Esther had to decide which king had her first allegiance—the king of Persia or God. She had to believe that God was with her and that this was the true reason for her success.

A series of happy "coincidences" followed. Haman asked Xerxes to honor him but was instead humiliated. Esther bravely defied the king's rules, and he liked her for it. Haman was hanged. The Jews were saved. Mordecai became the chief nobleman.

God was in charge, I told the class. He showed himself to be the better King. Haman should have sought honor from God instead of from Xerxes. And Esther proved herself wise for trusting God first.

"She must have been tempted to trust all the rich things Xerxes could give her," I said. "We get tempted that way too. We think the world's treasures are better than God's. Like Esther, we need to remember we're God's people. We have a far better King than even the great king of Persia. Our King is worth putting first."

Then one by one, we went back over the events of the story pictured on the whiteboard. We looked at them in light of *our* King, Jesus:

- The king of Persia ruled an empire. But King Jesus rules all heaven and earth.
- King Jesus can't be duped by a gift to his treasury. He owns all things and freely shares them with us.
- King Jesus won't love us for a night, use us for his pleasure, and then let us go. He gives us a costly love that's faithful forever.
- And King Jesus doesn't execute all traitors. Every one of us has been unfaithful to him. We've plotted against him and deserve to die. But he has gone to the gallows in our place, shedding his blood, impaled at his hands and feet.

"There's no king like our King," I said. "He controls all things and defends his people, so trust him. Remember who you are and who you serve. It will make you wise and brave like Esther."

We finished by discussing places that can be like Esther's harem— school, sports teams, being with friends. The kids gave examples of how each of these seduces them, promising happiness if kids will conform. It was a good discussion.

I thought it was over—until the mom spoke up. She had something to add. The kids should know, she said, that the pressure only gets worse as you get older. Every job she'd ever had was like that harem. They had tried to force her to fit in and do things certain ways that weren't God's way. The kids should remember this lesson, she told them. They must never forget they have a better King.

That word from a parent seemed to get through to the kids. The mom had given a perfect end to the lesson. I admit, though, that I was mostly just relieved she didn't mind the bodies on the gallows.

ONE STORY ABOUT JESUS

I know only two ways to teach the Esther story that will please a mom. One is to skip the sex and violence. The other is to exit through the cross.

If I'd used the Esther story merely to teach a moral lesson such as "be brave" or "help God's people," it actually would have worked better to edit the Bible's version of the account. That right there should tell us the Bible isn't meant to be turned into neat, isolated moral lessons.

The Bible is one epic story about God saving his people. We can't rightly understand any part of it unless we understand that context. This epic story centers on the person and work of Jesus. If we cut individual stories off from the Bible's central story arc about Jesus, we miss the main thing the Bible wants to say—and fashion Bible stories that aren't biblical.

The Bible is the word of God because it's about *the* Word, Jesus. We're sons of God because we're in *the* Son, also Jesus. We must never bypass Jesus when applying the Bible to our lives. To do so fits neither the Bible nor us.

When Jesus explained to his disciples how all the Bible is about him, he said, "Thus it is written, that the Christ should suffer and on the third day rise from the dead, and that repentance and forgiveness of sins should be proclaimed in his name to all nations, beginning from Jerusalem" (Luke 24:46–47). Not only is the whole Bible about Jesus, but Jesus says it's more specifically all about the good news— his death and resurrection, and repentance and forgiveness of sin. All Bible paths lead there.

THE FIRST CHRISTIAN TEACHERS

The book of Acts gives three detailed examples of how Christian teachers instruct from the Bible. These examples are in the form of sermons that are among the least studied parts of the whole book. We tend to skip over them. They feel like a rehash of stories we've heard before. But we should slow down and take notes. In each case the Bible teacher shows how the stories and truths of the Bible are supposed to lead us to Jesus and the good news.

- In Acts 2, Peter preaches about the prophets who told of salvation and about David, who wrote in the Psalms of an undying King. He then tells how David "foresaw and spoke about the resurrection of the Christ" (Acts 2:31).
- In Acts 7, Stephen preaches about the sufferings of God's people and the salvation they received, telling Bible story after Bible story from Abraham to Solomon and the prophets. Then he tells how Jesus is the ultimate suffering prophet, "the Righteous One, whom you have now betrayed and murdered" (Acts 7:52).
- In Acts 13, Paul preaches about God's care, using Bible stories about Moses, Joshua, Samuel, Saul, and David. Paul then tells how God has most fully cared for all people by giving forgiveness through Jesus: "We bring you the good news that what God promised to the fathers, this he has fulfilled to us their children by raising Jesus" (Acts 13:32–33).

Oddly, the story passages used so effectively by teachers *in* the Bible are largely neglected in adult teaching *of* the Bible in many churches today. You mostly hear them in classes for kids. This puts a responsibility on us who teach those lessons because our classrooms may be the most likely place in the whole church to hear the storyline that leads to Jesus. We must teach those stories the way teachers in the Bible did, with our eyes on the Savior.

God's Story, Their Story

I need to say that sometimes Bible characters *do* provide helpful moral lessons. In fact, I used the Esther story in this chapter partly because Esther *is* a good example to follow. I believe part of the reason the Esther story is in the Bible is to inspire us to be brave like she was. The story is also less obviously connected to the main salvation story arc than are many other Old Testament passages—but do you see that *even then*, the lesson is stronger when it's tied to the good news? Focusing on God's saving work and on Jesus made the lesson most motivating.

With many other stories it's the only approach that holds together. Take Jacob, for example. Every group I've ever taught has been able to see how Jacob just doesn't work as a moral example. He's faithful to God but dishonest. He trusts God but also schemes unnecessarily. He loves his wife—well, one of them—but plays favorites with his kids. So the best thing to say about Jacob is not that he's a good guy or a bad guy, but that he's God's guy. His life story is about God's goodness amid the mess.

This is how Jesus saw the lives of people he met. The Gospels rarely show him telling a character to behave. More often, he commends them for their faith in him or expresses disappointment for their lack of it. There are two examples of Jesus being amazed. One is Matthew 8:10, where a Roman centurion has faith that Jesus can heal by speaking. The other is Mark 6:6, where the people of Nazareth *don't* believe. In both cases the central issue is faith. The characters' responses to what *God* is doing is far more important than what *they're* doing.

Anywhere you turn in the Bible, God's saving work forms the backdrop. Laws, prophecies, poems—all exist within the story of salvation. The good news is the Bible's drumbeat. To ignore it at any point is to misplay the theme song.

How Jesus Taught the Hard Lessons

An excellent teacher I know once decided to teach three lessons to a group of teenagers, all from consecutive chapters in Mark. The first week she taught from chapter 8, where Jesus first tells his disciples about his impending death and resurrection: "And he began to teach them that the Son of Man must suffer many things and be rejected by the elders and the chief priests and the scribes and be killed, and after three days rise again" (Mark 8:31). She also taught what comes right after that, where Jesus issues one of the strongest calls to whole-hearted obedience found anywhere in the Bible: "If anyone would come after me, let him deny himself and take up his cross and follow me. For whoever would save his life will lose it, but whoever loses his life for my sake and the gospel's will save it" (Mark 8:34–35). That was lesson one.

The next week she taught from the next chapter, where Jesus says, "The Son of Man is going to be delivered into the hands of men, and they will kill him. And when he is killed, after three days he will rise" (Mark 9:31). She then taught what comes after that—another hard teaching: "If anyone would be first, he must be last of all and servant of all" (Mark 9:35). Lesson two.

The third week showed Jesus approaching Jerusalem and steadily walking ahead of his disciples, who are scared. He tells them, "See, we are going up to Jerusalem, and the Son of Man will be delivered over to the chief priests and the scribes, and they will condemn him to death and deliver him over to the Gentiles. And they will mock him and spit on him, and flog him and kill him. And after three days he will rise" (Mark 10:33–34).

The students were getting tired of what seemed like the same lesson, but the teacher showed how Jesus used that moment to again drive home yet another hard teaching: "Whoever would be great among you must be your servant, and whoever would be first among you must be slave of all. For even the Son of Man came not to be served but to serve, and to give his life as a ransom for many" (Mark 10:43–45). Lesson three.

That teacher was smart. She wanted her students to never forget that Jesus's instructions in the Bible—especially his most difficult ones—do not come in a vacuum. They happen in the context of his determination to die for us. His march toward the cross is a major theme in every one of the Gospels. A wise teacher never loses this context—never lets Jesus's comments be cut off from his cross.

From Redemption to Response

God's commands have always flowed from his saving work, all the way back to Mount Sinai. How do the Ten Commandments and the rest of the Law of Moses begin? With God reminding his people how he saved them: "I am the LORD your God, who brought you out of the land of Egypt, out of the house of slavery. You shall have no other gods before me" (Exodus 20:2–3).

How were kids in those days taught to follow God's law? Moses said to do it by telling the story of how God saved his people: "When your son asks you in time to come, 'What is the meaning of the testimonies and the statutes and the rules that the LORD our God has commanded you?' then you shall say to your son, 'We were Pharaoh's slaves in Egypt. And the LORD brought us out of Egypt with a mighty hand'" (Deuteronomy 6:20–21). It should come as no surprise, then, that once God's saving work reaches its peak in Jesus, the Bible constantly uses this salvation to motivate us.

Many New Testament epistles follow a pattern of first telling the good news, then showing how to live in response. The book of Romans starts with eleven whole chapters of good news. Among other things, we read that God has called us to himself (1:6), given us righteousness (3:22), justified us (3:24), given us peace with God (5:1), made us dead to sin and alive to God (6:11), given us life in the Spirit (7:6), adopted us as his sons (8:15), assured us of glory (8:18), loved us forever (8:38–39), chosen us as his people (9:25), removed our shame (10:11), and granted us mercy (11:32).

Whew! That's a ton of good news. And it's only *after* all that setup that the Bible gives instructions for how to live in response to that good news: "I appeal to you therefore, brothers, by the mercies of God, to present your bodies as a living sacrifice, holy and acceptable to God, which is your spiritual worship" (Romans 12:1). The rest of the book is mostly how-you-should-live instructions.

Our custom of taking the Bible a verse at a time means that we often miss this pattern. We think there's doctrine (stuff about what

God does for us in Jesus) and instruction (what we must do for God). We fail to see how they're connected. We ought to teach them together. We should teach the good news with an urgency and expectation that its payoff is good behavior, or else our doctrine will be served cold. And we must teach good behavior only when we show it flowing from the good news, or else kids will choke on moralism.

Looking more closely at the Epistles verse by verse, the good news is a constant way of motivating good behavior. Consider some examples:

- *How are we motivated to be generous?* By the good news. Jesus has been generous to us. "For you know the grace of our Lord Jesus Christ, that though he was rich, yet for your sake he became poor, so that you by his poverty might become rich" (2 Corinthians 8:9).
- *How are we motivated to stay sexually pure?* By the good news. Jesus has redeemed our bodies. "Do you not know that your body is a temple of the Holy Spirit within you, whom you have from God? You are not your own, for you were bought with a price. So glorify God in your body" (1 Corinthians 6:19–20).
- *How are we motivated to forgive each other?* By the good news. Jesus forgives us. "Be kind to one another, tenderhearted, forgiving one another, as God in Christ forgave you" (Ephesians 4:32).
- *How are we motivated to love?* By the good news. God sent his Son to die for us. "Beloved, if God so loved us, we also ought to love one another" (1 John 4:11).
- *How are we motivated to stop evil sins?* By the good news. We have a glorious future with Jesus. "When Christ who is your life appears, then you also will appear with him in glory. Put to death therefore what is earthly in you: sexual immorality, impurity, passion, evil desire, and covetousness, which is idolatry" (Colossians 3:4–5).

- *How are we motivated to lay down our lives for each other?*
  By the good news. Jesus laid down his life for us. "By this we
  know love, that he laid down his life for us, and we ought to
  lay down our lives for the brothers" (1 John 3:16).

There are dozens of these passages. I've only given a sample of
some of the shorter ones. I hope you can see how the Bible writers'
pattern is to tap into gospel power. The things they command are hard
to do, but they can boldly call Christians to live that way because they
ground their teaching in the good news.

The practical value of this is huge. Do we dream of Christian kids
who are generous? Sexually pure? Forgiving? Laying down their lives
for others? If so, we have a model for ministry that comes straight
from the apostles. We must be honest about the ugliness of sin. We
must teach kids not to rely on willpower but to have faith in God. And
we must unpack and parade before them the splendor of Jesus, the
crucified and risen Christ.

QUESTIONS YOU MIGHT BE ASKING

*You seem awfully willing to include sex and violence in Bible stories
for young kids. Is that wise?*

I'm sure there have been times that I made the wrong decision
about how much kids can handle. Often I do tone down the sex and
violence in a Bible story to fit the age of the kids. It's good to protect
kids to some extent and to let parents take the lead in deciding what
their kids should be exposed to. Other times, especially in the case of
violence, I go ahead and tell what the Bible tells for the following two
reasons:

1. It's good to remain as faithful as possible to the whole Bible
   account because that's how God gave it.
2. It's better if kids' early exposure to the cruelty of this world
   comes through the Bible, where God's story of healing and
   forgiveness is also told. It may be hard to discover violence

in the Bible, but it's much harder to discover it *without* the Bible. I let kids see how God is in control of death and pain and even man's cruelty, and is rescuing us from these things in Jesus. The Bible *is* blood-stained. Its accounts of sin and gruesomeness are a serious barrier to teaching it to kids unedited. I see no reason to subject them to any of it *unless* I'm using it to teach about the blood of Jesus.

I'm not convinced that drawing moral lessons from a Bible character's life is wrong. Teachers have done that for centuries. Is it really all that bad?

Sometimes it *is* that bad—when we force moral lessons that are barely supported by the text or not there at all. One of the thickest books I own is a guide to all the New Testament passages that refer to the Old Testament.[2] Only a handful of those are passages where an Old Testament character is used as an example of how to live. If we teach Old Testament lessons that are *mostly* how-to-live examples, we're taking a different approach than the Bible itself takes.

On other occasions, it's good and proper. Jesus used Lot's wife, who turned back when fleeing Sodom, as an example for disciples to be ready to abandon worldly goods when his kingdom comes: "Remember Lot's wife. Whoever seeks to preserve his life will lose it, but whoever loses his life will keep it" (Luke 17:32–33). Paul used the destruction of many Israelites in the wilderness as another example: "Now these things took place as examples for us, that we might not desire evil as they did. Do not be idolaters as some of them were" (1 Corinthians 10:6–7).

Bible characters *can* be behavioral examples. That's part of God's salvation plan too. He's worked in the lives of real people we can learn from. Just don't leave out God's role in the story. If you study the context of these two passages, you'll find they're still tied to salvation and the need to believe the good news, which both Jesus and Paul are most concerned with.

So are you saying that when we teach our children to be godly, we should always teach the good news first?

The sequence isn't the main thing. Do remember that God's grace toward us never depends on us having earned it by being good. In that sense God's kindness always comes first. But don't let that stifle your style. When we teach, we have freedom to present this in many ways. Although the Bible often tells of God's grace first, it also switches things around. Sometimes it'll tell Christians what to do and then remind them of what God has already done. The main thing is not to neglect the good news. I sometimes open my lessons with it, sometimes close with it, and often weave it in at many spots throughout.

I understand some Old Testament passages are prophecies about Jesus. But aren't you going too far in saying it's all about Jesus?

I'm only saying what the Bible says about itself. Every part—all of it—witnesses to Jesus. The Bible uses "all" language on this issue. There's Jesus with his disciples: "And beginning with Moses and all the Prophets, he interpreted to them in all the Scriptures the things concerning himself" (Luke 24:27). Notice Luke's use of "all." Then there's Peter preaching at the temple: "But what God foretold by the mouth of all the prophets, that his Christ would suffer, he thus fulfilled" (Acts 3:18). Peter tells how Moses spoke of Jesus, then says again, "All the prophets who have spoken, from Samuel and those who came after him, also proclaimed these days" (Acts 3:24). Then later with Cornelius, Peter says, "To him all the prophets bear witness that everyone who believes in him receives forgiveness of sins through his name" (Acts 10:43). All, all, all.

Not every verse mentions Jesus directly. But every part of the Bible contributes to the all-about-Jesus theme, and we need to read it that way. If you still need convincing, look up the following verses that tell how Jesus is not just the fulfillment of specific prophecies but is the theme of the whole Old Testament. I know it's a long list, but that's the point!

- Matthew 5:17; 26:54
- Mark 9:12; 14:49
- Luke 1:70; 16:29–31; 18:31; 21:22
- John 1:45; 5:39
- Acts 17:2, 11; 18:28; 24:14; 26:22–23
- Romans 1:1–3; 3:21; 16:25–26
- 1 Corinthians 15:3–4
- 2 Timothy 3:15
- 1 Peter 1:10–12
- Revelation 10:7

What about the original intent of Old Testament authors? Aren't you unfair to them when you read your Jesus interpretation into a passage written by a guy who never heard of Jesus?

It's hard to know the intent of an author who wrote several thousand years ago. But there are two things we know for sure because the Bible tells us.

1. The Old Testament authors, inspired by the Holy Spirit, did have some knowledge of Jesus and meant to write about the good news. "The prophets who prophesied about the grace that was to be yours searched and inquired carefully, inquiring what person or time the Spirit of Christ in them was indicating when he predicted the sufferings of Christ and the subsequent glories. It was revealed to them that they were serving not themselves but you, in the things that have now been announced to you through those who preached the good news to you" (1 Peter 1:10–12). Those authors knew they were part of something bigger than the immediate context of their writings. As such, they knew something of the sufferings and glories of Jesus. They wrote for the benefit of later Christians. Jesus put it even more plainly: "For if you believed Moses, you would believe me; for he wrote of me" (John 5:46).

2. There are two authors to every book of the Bible—the human author and the Holy Spirit. The human author's intent may be partly unknown, but we know the passion and purpose of the Spirit. It is to glorify and bear witness to Jesus (see John 15:26, 16:14). This he has done in all of the pages of Scripture.

I don't reinterpret what the Old Testament writers said. I try first to be true to what they said and to the good news as they could see it—then bring their story forward to include the fuller view of Jesus we have today. We'll learn more about this technique in the next chapter.

Show Them Jesus Right Away

Here are some ways you can get started connecting everything you teach from the Bible to the good news of Jesus:

Parents: When your kids ask, "Why do we follow these rules God gives us?" be ready to answer them the way Moses directed—by telling of God's saving work. Take a few minutes *now* to anticipate godly behaviors your kids might challenge or complain about, like letting others go first, contentment with less, or sexual purity. Write down now what you plan to say about Jesus so you'll be ready. For example, "We let others go first *because Jesus saved us to be different from the world*. He put his personal interests last for our sake—even dying for us. We do the same for others." Practice frequently connecting Christian behavior to the good news, rather than merely saying, "God says it (or *I* say it), so do it!"

Teachers: Replace one of your standard lessons with one of the Bible lessons taught in Acts. The easiest one to use is Paul's talk in Antioch from Acts 13:16–41. Use it as the outline for your lesson instead of something from a teacher's guide. By doing so you'll touch on Bible stories, psalms, and prophecies from Exodus all the way through to the New Testament, showing your students how these portions of the Bible lead to Jesus and urging your class to believe in him. If you usually use published lessons, this lesson will likely be quite different from that norm—but straight out of the Bible's own lesson book.

Anyone: Decorate your classroom, camp, youth room, or home with handmade posters that connect godly behavior to the good news.

Write down, "Why _____?" and quote a verse that connects that behavior to what Jesus has done for us. Here are some examples:

- *Why share?* "For you know the grace of our Lord Jesus Christ, that though he was rich, yet for your sake he became poor, so that you by his poverty might become rich" (2 Corinthians 8:9).
- *Why stay pure?* "You are not your own, for you were bought with a price. So glorify God in your body" (1 Corinthians 6:19–20).
- *Why forgive?* "Be kind to one another, tenderhearted, forgiving one another, as God in Christ forgave you" (Ephesians 4:32).
- *Why be kind?* "Walk in love, as Christ loved us and gave himself up for us" (Ephesians 5:2).

Have your kids help make the posters and put them up as constant reminders that our connection to Jesus is why we obey God. (If merely mentioning godly behavior makes your kids feel guilty, consider adding a banner to go above the whole display with a verse reminding them that those who are in Christ don't need to fear God's law—perhaps 1 John 2:12: "Your sins are forgiven for his name's sake.")

Section Two

How to Teach the Good News

Chapter 6

The Talking Donkey and Jesus

Teaching the good news from the Old Testament

Christ is the treasure hid in the field of the scriptures,
the water in those wells.
—Matthew Henry1

Every now and then I teach a class for the whole family. This lets little kids, teenagers, their parents, and even grandparents attend and learn together. This is helpful to many families, so there's much that I like about teaching these intergenerational classes. Sometimes, though, I obsess over picking just the right topic or Bible story.

Not long ago, I was a few weeks away from an upcoming family class. I mentioned this to a group of young kids. They wanted to know what Bible story I'd be teaching. "I haven't decided yet," I told them. Big mistake.

"Oh, I know what story you should teach," one of them said.

"What's that?"

"The one with the talking donkey!"

Before I could protest, the rest of the kids were agreeing. "Yes, teach us about the talking donkey. Pleeeease!"

I told them I'd consider it, which was not much different from saying yes. I was committed. Any other lesson would now be a disappointment. But it'd been years since I'd taught about the sorcerer

Balaam, who hoped to put a curse on the Israelites and traveled to the job on his donkey—with amusing results. I couldn't remember if I'd ever taught that story with the gospel in mind.

Now I had to teach a good-news lesson about Balaam. I'd have to figure out what that talking donkey had to do with Jesus.

A Few Simple Questions

Before we begin walking through this process together, let me say this: If you teach Bible lessons, you *do* need to come up with your own lesson content. Even if you use published lessons—even if they're good, Jesus-centered lessons—you still need to set them down for a time. You need to go through the process of studying, thinking, and finding wonder in Jesus for yourself.

You might end up using much of what your teacher's guide says. Still, the best teaching moments seldom come from following a script someone else has prepared, even a good script. They come from excitedly teaching rich truths you've discovered for yourself—and that discovery takes some work. For the Balaam lesson, I spent time learning the context of the story. In that sense the lesson prep was hard. However, connecting Balaam's story to Jesus didn't require any obscure Bible knowledge or moment of brilliance; it was fairly easy. You could do it too.

Let me show you how I connected Balaam with Jesus. I pick this lesson partly because it didn't end up having any particularly clever insights. Getting to the good news from an Old Testament story usually isn't about being clever; it's about approaching the story with the right questions. Here's the set of questions I used to tackle the Balaam story:

- What is *God* doing for his people in this story?
- Good news! How does God do the same for us—only better—in Jesus?
- Believe it! How does believing this good news change how we live?

Of course, I also needed to decide how to present these themes in a way that was clear and interesting. That's good technique, and you should use what works for you. But the lesson *content* itself was just the answers to these three questions. Not complicated at all.

BALAAM AND HIS DONKEY

We started by looking at where Balaam appears in the book of Numbers, more than a thousand years before Jesus. The Israelites were ready to enter the land of Canaan and drive out the people there. Centuries before, God had promised their ancestor Abraham he'd give it to them. He also promised prosperity and protection: "I will bless those who bless you, and whoever curses you I will curse" (Genesis 12:3, NIV 1984).

Enter Balaam. The king of nearby Moab was scared of the Israelites and decided to hire the region's most powerful sorcerer to curse the people. He offered Balaam much money and praised his talent at witchcraft: "I know that he whom you bless is blessed, and he whom you curse is cursed" (Numbers 22:6). There's the setup. They can't both be right. Is God's promise trustworthy, or is the king right about Balaam's evil powers?

Oh yes, Balaam is a bad guy. My class noticed points in the story where he looks like a good man, asking God for approval before taking action. But when you're offered a pile of money to hurt someone, "I'll pray about it" is not a good answer. Balaam *wanted* to curse the people. He loved the money he'd get. So he headed out on his donkey, hoping to do evil.

A dangerous curse was headed toward God's people. Cue the scary music.

Then God came down. The angel of the Lord took his stand in the road in front of Balaam, sword drawn to kill him. Balaam—the supposed spiritual genius in this story—couldn't see the angel, but his donkey did. The donkey veered off the road and through a field, and Balaam hit her to get her back on track. Later the angel returned and this time the donkey moved to the side, pressing Balaam's foot against a wall. He hit her again. The third time the angel appeared the donkey just sat down in the road. Balaam, embarrassed at losing control of his animal, beat her with his staff.

> Then the LORD opened the mouth of the donkey, and she said to Balaam, "What have I done to you, that you have struck me these three times?" And Balaam said to the donkey, "Because you have made a fool of me. I wish I had a sword in my hand, for then I would kill you." And the donkey said to Balaam, "Am I not your donkey, on which you have ridden all your life long to this day? Is it my habit to treat you this way?" And he said, "No." (Numbers 22:28–30)

I asked the class, "What's happening to Balaam here?" They smiled. Some chuckled. A few offered comments on how silly Balaam looked. All understood that it wasn't the donkey, but God, who was making mighty Balaam into an even bigger clown than he realized. He'd gone on a stupid-looking ride through a field. He'd hurt his poor foot. Now he was arguing with a donkey—and the donkey was winning. Ha! What a dope!

Just look what happens to big shots who try to curse people God has blessed.

When God opened Balaam's eyes, he saw the angel and fell on his face. He offered to turn back, but the angel told him to go ahead—and speak only words God would give him. That's how Balaam, who'd come to curse, instead blessed the Israelites in a series of oracles. "A star shall come out of Jacob, and a scepter shall rise out of Israel; it shall crush the forehead of Moab" (Numbers 24:17).

MAKING THE CONNECTION

I asked the class to discuss what God did for his people in the story. There were plenty of answers: "He kept an evil man from hurting them." "He made bad things happen to the guy who was cursing them, just like he promised." "He made a joke out of what threatened them."

"He showed them he's stronger than their enemies." Those were all good answers, and I said so.

We then read from Deuteronomy 23:5, where the Bible itself comments on what God did: "But the LORD your God would not listen to Balaam; instead the LORD your God turned the curse into a blessing for you, because the LORD your God loved you." And on the board, I wrote out "God stops the curse and lovingly gives blessings instead."

"Look at it," I said. "What does this story mean for us, thousands of years later, as people who belong to Jesus? Has God done anything like this for us too?"

I had to wait a moment, but soon the answers started coming. A teenager was first. "God gives us lots of blessings because he loves us," he said.

A parent built on that: "We deserve to be cursed," she said. "We're sinners and we were going to get the curse of hell. But Jesus came and stopped it and took our curse and gives us blessings instead."

"We can laugh because of what he's done for us," another observed.

I let the discussion continue for a few more minutes, but the point had been made. Jesus stopped the worst curse of all, forever, by dying for our sin. I read from Colossians 2:13–15. "He forgave us all our sins, having canceled the written code, with its regulations, that was against us and that stood opposed to us; he took it away, nailing it to the cross. And having disarmed the powers and authorities, he made a public spectacle of them, triumphing over them by the cross" (NIV 1984).

We ended by talking about how the cross means that the enemies we fear are being put to shame—being made a public spectacle like Balaam. I asked how our behavior would change if we fully believed this. One guy shared how he'd dare to stick up for what's right at work. A kid said she'd start to feel bad for the mean girls at school instead of just hating them.

We'd connected the talking donkey to life in Jesus.

THE QUESTIONS ANSWERED

Let's look back at the questions I started with.

What is *God* doing for his people in this story? *He stops the curse and lovingly gives blessings instead.* There were several good ways to answer this question, but I chose to highlight the one emphasized by the Bible itself.

Good news! How does God do the same for us—only better—in Jesus? *By dying for our sins, Jesus stops the worst curse of all. He has taken the curse we deserve and gives us every blessing instead.* You may think this answer is obvious, but in my lesson prep it took me five or ten minutes of thinking about curses before I saw it. When I asked the question in class, someone else came up with the answer in less than a minute.

Believe it! How does believing this good news change how we live? *We dare to stick up for what's right at work. We can love our enemies instead of fearing them.* I came into class with my own thoughts on this, but I ended up going with what the group wanted to share. If the class had been only young kids, I probably would have had to suggest something. I was prepared to discuss scary kinds of people and situations that make us doubt God, and how they aren't so scary when you consider the Balaam story—and Jesus.

ONE BASIC PRINCIPLE

That's it. So don't be intimidated. Yes, some people spend years learning the fine points of Old Testament interpretation. I'm all for that, but most of us who teach kids haven't been able to go to seminary. We can still teach the Old Testament.

Jesus set down the basic principle on one afternoon walk lasting no more than a few hours. The day he rose from the dead he walked with two disciples to the town of Emmaus. They didn't understand his death and resurrection, and he scolded them for it: "O foolish ones, and slow of heart to believe all that the prophets have spoken!" (Luke 24:25). Then he explained how all the Old Testament leads to him.

Jesus. He's the principle for teaching the Old Testament. It's so simple and clear that Jesus called those disciples unbelieving fools for missing it. Seeing Jesus in the Old Testament isn't some deep prophecy stuff for those teachers who are ultra-scholarly. It's the ABCs. You'll be on the right basic track—and well ahead of the two disciples—just by teaching the Old Testament with one eye on Jesus. It's that easy.

KEEP IT SIMPLE

Of course, we still want to teach Jesus with the best possible under-standing of the Bible. But for most of us, most of the time, this means keeping it simple.

You may think a Bible story can't lead to Jesus unless you find a direct prophecy about him. Well, the Old Testament does contain many such prophecies, but they aren't everywhere. Most story passages don't have one. Don't force it.

As it turns out, the Balaam passage is one of those rare Old Testament stories that *does* contain a direct prophecy about Jesus. Balaam's oracle about a star and scepter to come from the Israelites is a reference to the Messiah. When I prepped my lesson, I knew I could connect Balaam to Jesus this way, but I also knew it wasn't the only connection in the passage. I chose instead to focus on how God stopped the curse, knowing that it too led to good points about Jesus.

So if, despite little training, you find yourself teaching Bible stories at church or leading family devotions, don't worry about trying to find specific prophecies about Jesus. If you come across one, you can use it. But you don't *need* one in order to teach the good news.

It's the same with a "type." That's what Bible scholars call a person, thing, or event in the Old Testament that's a symbolic picture of Jesus and foreshadows him. King David is a type for Jesus—a shadow of the ultimate Shepherd King. The Passover lamb is also a type—prefiguring the Innocent One who died to save us. Types are fun to think about, and God arranged biblical events so as to provide many of them.

Maybe you're well-trained enough to find a type for Jesus in a Bible passage and want to teach it that way. Excellent. The New

Testament writers did a lot of this. But again, you don't *need* one to get to Jesus. Nor should you force one.

What if I'd been trying to get clever with the Balaam story and find a type? Is the angel a picture of Jesus, who fights for his people? Does the sword foreshadow Jesus, whose words are sharp and pointed? Maybe the donkey stands for Jesus, who speaks hidden truths our eyes cannot see. Or are these attempts to be *too* clever?

I could make a case for the angel. The angel of the Lord is a character who appears often in the Old Testament and acts a lot like Jesus—so much so that some Bible experts think he *is* Jesus. But I didn't go there in my Balaam lesson. I liked my simpler, stop-the-curse theme. And I surely didn't want to look too hard and end up making a sad mistake like teaching that Balaam's donkey is a picture of Jesus.

Jesus is all over the Balaam story. We don't need cute tricks to draw him out. It doesn't require an "aha" moment where we reveal it was all about Jesus. We aren't trying to look fancy.

Just notice how God is working. Then expand. Complete it with Jesus. *Every* Old Testament story is unfinished without him.

METHOD #1: WHAT GOD DOES

Many of us, when trying to teach kids, are used to thinking first about the *human* characters in a Bible story. We find an example from them, good or bad, and that's our lesson. It's me-centered, not God-centered.

Imagine the poor teacher who tries to make an example out of Balaam. Balaam is a morally conflicted mess. He ends up doing exactly what God says, but his original intent was evil. Do you make him a fine example of obedience or a hard lesson about what happens to God's enemies? I suspect this dilemma is why this fine story about God's protection has largely disappeared from published children's lessons today. We don't know what to say because we're focused on the wrong character.

The main character in the Balaam story isn't Balaam. It's God. To focus on Balaam trivializes God's work in the story. So here's the first rule of teaching from the Old Testament:

Don't: Look for a moral lesson about a human character.

Instead: Look for the worth and work of the main character, God.

Again, start with the question *What is God doing for his people?* It's important to take your time with the answer. Learn the context of the Old Testament story. Know what comes before and after. Consider how God is working in the lives of the human characters. It's a bit different with each story and each character, and this is what gives freshness to each lesson. Don't be too quick to flip over to Jesus for just another bland mention of the cross. First find the richness of God's work in the Old Testament story. That way, with each story you teach you can turn to Jesus with a unique way to appreciate him.

Let's see how we might apply our set of questions to some familiar Old Testament stories.

LESSON: Baby Moses

What is God doing for his people in this story? He arranges events to protect baby Moses and give the Israelites a leader who will rescue them from Egypt.

Good news! How does God do the same for us—only better—in Jesus? He has provided a Leader and Savior who rescues us from sin and death.

Believe it! How does believing this good news change how we live? Even when it's hard to see, we can trust that God is working out his plan to complete our salvation.

LESSON: The Ten Commandments

What is God doing for his people in this story? He comes down to make the Israelites his holy nation, giving his Law to show them how to be holy.

Good news! How does God do the same for us—only better—in Jesus? He has come down as Jesus to bring us into God's kingdom. Jesus has kept God's law for us and made us holy.

Believe it! How does believing this good news change how we live? As people belonging to God, we're eager and able to obey his laws and proclaim his excellencies (1 Peter 2:9).

LESSON: Gideon

What is God *doing for his people in this story?* He chooses a weak man with a weak army to save the Israelites.

Good news! How does God do the same for us—only better—in Jesus? Through the weakness of Jesus, he chooses to save us who are weak in the world (1 Corinthians 1:27).

Believe it! How does believing this good news change how we live? We do not boast. We are content in hardships and weakness, knowing that faith in God beats worldly strength.

LESSON: Hannah

What is God *doing for his people in this story?* He answers Hannah's prayer and cares about her problems. He turns her from a despised person into one with a big role in his work.

Good news! How does God do the same for us—only better—in Jesus? Jesus cares when we have problems. He takes the despised people of this world and makes them his people.

Believe it! How does believing this good news change how we live? We pray with confidence in Christ, sure that he cares about our problems and will do far more through us than all we ask or think (Ephesians 3:20).

LESSON: Jonah

What is God *doing for his people in this story?* He shows grace and compassion to all kinds of people, from a disobedient prophet to the enemies in Nineveh.

Good news! How does God do the same for us—only better—in Jesus? In Jesus, God's saving compassion extends to the whole world. All of us—from churchy hypocrites to outright rebels— are enemies saved by grace.

Believe it! How does believing this good news change how we live? We rejoice! We realize how improbable our salvation is and give all credit to our compassionate God.

Again, these steps just get you the pieces of your lesson. You won't necessarily teach those pieces in this order every time; that would get boring. Plus, always ending with how we live might give kids the wrong idea that Christianity is chiefly about how well they perform, no matter how strongly you stress the good news first.

Notice, though, that starting with God doesn't mean the lesson has no behavior application—nor does bringing in Jesus mean the Old Testament point gets left behind. This method stays true to the message of the Old Testament passage. Including the good news of Jesus only makes the original point even richer.

Most stories include several things God is doing. The themes I've picked to emphasize in my examples are not the only options. To pick a good one it helps to keep in mind some of the main themes of God's work in history. He creates and sustains life. He fights evil. He defends the helpless. He chooses people to be his own. He lives among them. He makes and keeps covenants. He declares his law. He gives grace. He reveals himself in his Word. He displays his majesty. He defends his name. He champions justice. He rules the nations. He raises up rescuers and kings. He saves from sin and death. He provides rest. He protects. He heals. He speaks. He disciplines. He forgives. He loves.

METHOD #2: WHO GOD IS

Instead of focusing on what God is doing, sometimes it's simpler just to notice his character and goodness. Especially if you're teaching older kids and moving beyond the Bible's story passages, God's character may be an easier starting place. So we might change our questions a bit.

- What does this Bible passage teach us about *who God is*?
- Good news! How is this aspect of God revealed—most fully—in Jesus?
- Believe it! How does believing this good news change how we live?

We could use these questions to prepare lessons on stories and passages like the following:

LESSON: Psalm 23

What does this Bible passage teach us about who God is? He is our shepherd, gently meeting our every need and protecting us from all dangers.

Good news! How is this aspect of God revealed—most fully— in Jesus? Jesus meets our greatest need of all by being the Good Shepherd, so loving that he laid down his life for the sheep (John 10:11).

Believe it! How does believing this good news change how we live? Knowing that Jesus went so far as to die for us, we are confident that we shall not want for any good thing. He will always be with us, and we fear no evil.

LESSON: The Golden Calf

What does this Bible passage teach us about who God is? Like any lover, he is a jealous God. He fiercely demands that his people worship him alone, in his way.

Good news! How is this aspect of God revealed—most fully—in Jesus? Jesus calls for his followers' *entire lives* to be wholly devoted to him. He's so jealous for us to be his alone that he died to redeem us from the devil.

Believe it! How does believing this good news change how we live? When we know how much Jesus longs to be with us forever, it makes us yearn to be with him too.

Again, there's so much in the Bible about God's majesty and character—all seen most fully in Jesus—that the possible topics seem endless. We can teach about his mercy, his power, his kindness, his justice, his determination to save, his eye for outcasts, and on and on and on.

METHOD #3: JESUS SOLVES PROBLEMS

The first two methods depend on how God's dealings with his people in the Old and New Testaments are much the same. But because the Old Testament anticipates Jesus, in some ways it also differs from the New. Its stories leave us unsettled.

The Bible's grand story unfolds as we progress from start to finish. With each turn it shows us more about the good news to come. Until we open the final fold and see Jesus, the whole picture never quite works. Old Testament stories tend to leave us with nagging problems or unsolved tensions, looking for more—for *him*. Read the prophets and you'll see that Old Testament believers sensed it too. They were able to carry on with God only because they had faith that he was doing something unseen and better.

Because of this, another way to teach Jesus from the Old Testament is to notice an unsolved problem or tension and then show how Jesus solves it.

- What problem/tension is left unsettled in this passage?
- Good news! How is this solved in Jesus?
- Believe it! How does believing this good news change how we live?

This set of questions opens up a whole new range of possibilities.

LESSON: Samson

What problem/tension is left unsettled in this passage? God uses Samson to save the Israelites from Philistine influence, yet Samson remains a flawed and unsatisfying savior for God's people.

Good news! How is this solved in Jesus? Only in Jesus do we find the flawless Savior we long for.

Believe it! How does believing this good news change how we live? We put our faith in Jesus alone, the only perfect Savior, knowing that in him God can use even flawed people like ourselves.

LESSON: The covenant at Mount Sinai

What problem/tension is left unsettled in this passage? God invites the Israelites into a covenant on the condition that they obey—how can they say no? But clearly they aren't able to obey, so how can they dare to say yes?

Good news! How is this solved in Jesus? In Jesus we're saved from both the guilt *and* the power of sin—forgiven *and* made able to obey.

Believe it! How does believing this good news change how we live? We dare to say yes to God with confidence and eagerness.

LESSON: Moses in the cleft of the rock

What problem/tension is left unsettled in this passage? Moses wants to see God's glory, but no sinful person can see God and live. So Moses must be satisfied with seeing God's back, not his face.

Good news! How is this solved in Jesus? In Jesus we have seen God's glory more fully than Moses did, yet in a form that brings us life rather than death. And one day we will see God's face (Revelation 22:4).

Believe it! How does believing this good news change how we live? We give up our puny desires for the lesser things of this world, setting our hopes on seeing more of Jesus.

The biggest tension in the Old Testament may be the one between God's love and his justice. It is stunningly resolved at the cross. Before that happens, however, it shows up in all sorts of Old Testament stories.

I once watched a kindergarten teacher tell the story of Noah without mentioning how all but eight people died in the flood or that it was God's judgment for sin. Now, that's understandable. Many children's books about Noah do the same. To protect youngsters, they're full of cute animals and rainbows and they never say that anyone got hurt.

But this teacher was bothered by what she'd done. She told me afterward that she'd struggled. She believed in teaching that God punishes those who don't obey, but in the case of the flood, the massive death toll just felt too ghastly—so she only told about the people God saved. Faced with the choice of making God out to be either a softie or a monster, she chose the kindhearted God.

Later, I thought about it and realized there's a third choice: *Tell the whole story* (always a good idea) *and acknowledge the tension.* God has to punish. He also loves to save. The flood is one of the many places where God's justice and mercy come together. So teach it something like the following:

LESSON: Noah and the flood

What problem/tension is left unsettled in this passage? God must punish sin but also loves to save. At the end he promises not to destroy the world again—but what will he do if people keep sinning?

Good news! How is this solved in Jesus? Jesus brings justice and mercy together. He suffered the punishment of God's justice for us so that now anyone who belongs to him—not just one family—is saved by God's mercy.

Believe it! How does believing this good news change how we live? We stop fearing God's judgment as we place our faith in the mercy that's ours in Jesus.

The only way to avoid either the softie God or the monster God is with the God of the cross. In fact, the New Testament does exactly this with the Noah story—see 1 Peter 3:18–21 for further evidence.

Teaching God's Commands

The Jesus-solves-problems framework also works for passages that spell out God's law. Many parts of the Old Testament tell how we must live. In these cases the problem is us. Like the Israelites who first heard these laws, the kids you teach will surely fail to keep them perfectly.

The good-news teacher welcomes such lessons. After all, our sin is the starting point for the good news (remember those Fs on the God Report Card?). It just means that when we teach any command, we *must* also stress how, already in the Old Testament, God made provision for sin and pointed to Jesus—who alone kept that command. I like to point out specific and amazing ways Jesus obeyed the exact command I'm teaching about, and that he also died for the way we break it. We're counted righteous when we're joined to him—as if we had obeyed as well as Jesus. Problem solved.

Except there's still more! The full good news regarding any of God's rules is that believers are (1) eternally *forgiven* for breaking that command and counted righteous in Jesus, no matter how badly they mess up; (2) *made eager* to follow that command in gratitude and hope as children of the Father; and (3) *made able* to follow it by relying on the Holy Spirit's transforming power. Never skip this good news. Teach it every time you teach God's commands.

> LESSON: Proverbs 14:5—"A faithful witness does not lie."
> *What problem/tension does this passage leave unsolved?* Telling the truth is both wise and commanded, but we often fail. We sin with our speech every day.
> *Good news! How does Jesus solve the problem?* Jesus did it! He controlled his speech perfectly. For example, he didn't get defensive at his trial even when witnesses lied about him, and he answered truthfully even when it meant being sentenced to die. When we're joined to him, he takes our failure and we get credit for his obedience.
> *Believe it! How does believing this good news change how we live?* We no longer feel condemned when we fail to speak truthfully. By trusting the Spirit, we're also eager and confident to speak more like Jesus.

Do you see how we take God's law seriously without it being a burden? It isn't about God deciding whether or not to love us, nor is it about anything we're stuck doing on our own. We *do* work at it, but in a trusting way that's part of life with God.

Because of this, a Christian kid who's rooted in the good news will *like* God's law. It will become a blessing in her life. She'll want to study it and do it, like the person in Psalm 1:2: "His delight is in the law of the LORD, and on his law he meditates day and night." (By the way, this verse too is a problem passage. It's made many a believer feel guilty or get worn out trying to measure up. Without Jesus, that verse is a burden. But in Jesus, the load is lifted, and this verse becomes true.)

Tip #1: Know the Big Story

I hope all these examples have shown you the importance of my first big tip for teaching any Old Testament lesson. It's an obvious but critical one: *a Bible teacher must know the Bible.* There's no getting around this. If you first learned Bible stories in isolated pieces, you need to learn how they fit together. The best method is just to read the Bible.

Before teaching any particular story, I usually read not only the passage itself but the surrounding chapters. If I haven't recently read the book of the Bible it's in, I might read that entire book. This, of course, is in addition to being generally familiar with the entire Old Testament. It's the only way I can properly see what God's doing in a story.

I know—that sounds time-consuming. I'm about to make it worse.

To connect the Old Testament to Jesus, you have to know all you can about Jesus too. This means knowing the New Testament even more thoroughly than the Old. It means reading through the Gospels and Epistles regularly, even when the passages you're teaching come from other parts of the Bible.

It does take time—but not that much compared to other things. I try to read through one of the Gospels or an epistle or two in one sitting every month. It takes less time than a movie, and I always notice new things to admire about Jesus.

I do this because it pays off. I'm not some super-spiritual guy who always has his nose stuck in the Bible for pious reasons (though it might be good if I were). In fact, for my first twenty years or so of Bible teaching I faked my way through discussions of Jesus, relying on my memory of stories I learned as a child. But now, I find that doing the reading makes me a better teacher and saves effort in the long run. For example, in my Balaam lesson I referred to Colossians 2:15 and how by the cross Jesus made a public spectacle of evil powers. That didn't come from any lesson guide or cross-reference notes; it just came to me as I was thinking about Balaam's embarrassment—and because a few months earlier, I'd reread Colossians.

TIP #2: CONSULT THE EXPERTS

Beyond knowing the Bible, I also trust those wiser than me to notice things I miss. Maybe you use a teacher's manual or devotional guide. If it's a good one, it'll give you some of the background and context to the story you're teaching. If it's a *very* good one, it'll show you how the theme you're teaching climaxes in Jesus.

If your lessons or family devotions don't contain some form of commentary, you can still use reference aids to get some of that information. Good ones will point you to other parts of the Bible that comment on the passage you're teaching. Even an ordinary reference Bible with related verses printed in the margins gets this done. In fact, it's how I realized that Deuteronomy provided commentary on the Balaam story.

A surprising number of popular Old Testament stories are directly mentioned in the New Testament—the Bible itself connects them to Jesus. For example, Jesus taught the story of manna in the wilderness and that God, who kept the Israelites alive with manna, now gives eternal life through Christ. "I am the living bread that came down from heaven" (John 6:51).

Another example is Paul teaching about the first day of creation. "For God, who said, 'Let light shine out of darkness,' has shone in our hearts to give the light of the knowledge of the glory of God in the face of Jesus Christ" (2 Corinthians 4:6). Elsewhere he mentions that Jesus was already at work on that first day. "For by him all things were created" (Colossians 1:16). Those aren't the only ways to get to Jesus from the creation story, but they're good ones that come straight from the Bible. Consult your reference aids because you don't want to miss connections like that.

Tip #3: Make It Work for Little Kids

I've already mentioned how keeping things simple is important. If you have young kids, or teach preschoolers, you know it matters doubly for them.

Take a story like the crossing of the Red Sea. They won't understand all the symbolism of how it foreshadows the cross of Jesus. Try to explain it like that, and little kids will think the connection has to do with the word "cross." Even if you make it easier and say something like, "God saved the Israelites through the sea, just like he saves us by Jesus dying on the cross," it still might make no sense. How is the cross like the Red Sea? There's no water in the cross story.

With this in mind I almost always stick to straight storytelling for the youngest kids: The Israelites were chased by the Egyptians. God saved them by making a path through the sea. He did this because he loves to save his people. He was getting ready for an even bigger kind of saving. Many years later Jesus saved lots of people from getting punished for their sin—he died on the cross to save people from that too.

It's that simple. Just tell the story and continue all the way to the good news.

Several years ago I had a class of preschoolers. I made a colorful card with the word "Jesus" printed on it and taught them to read it. I told them that all Bible stories led to Jesus. Then when I told my Old Testament stories, I'd get to a point where I said, "And many years later . . . ." That was the kids' cue to yell "Jesus!" as I reached for the card—and finished the story.

A repetitive approach like this wouldn't have worked with older kids, but it was just right for those preschoolers. They liked my little game. They also learned to look for Jesus wherever we started in the Bible. They were actually disappointed when we moved on to the New Testament—where Jesus was clearly in the story from the start.

Tip #4: Avoid "Bad God, Good God" Thinking

Finally, one thing *not* to do: Don't fall into the trap of thinking that the Bible's view of God changes in the New Testament. Never add a message about Jesus to an Old Testament lesson just to make those messy stories feel better and God look nicer.

Some people think the Old Testament God is vengeful or legalistic, so they prefer to emphasize love and sweetness by including Jesus. Others say that's the wrong move. They say you need to keep Jesus out of Old Testament lessons so as not to soften God's harsh side. Hogwash—all of it!

Both those views rest on the wrong assumption that the Old and New Testaments teach differing concepts of God. Don't make that mistake. God is the same throughout the Bible. If we think God isn't compassionate and forgiving in the Old Testament, we haven't read about his patience with the Israelites. And if we think he isn't demanding and warlike in the New Testament, we've missed some of Jesus's most pointed teaching—not to mention the book of Revelation. We've also been blind to the uncompromising violence of the cross.

The difference between the Old and New Testaments isn't the attributes of God they reveal, but the point we're at in the great story. The love of God that was always there and the demands that come with it are now visible in all their white-hot glory. As Christians who know Jesus, we teach with him in view—not to soften anything but to sharpen everything.

Years ago someone told me never to mention Jesus when teaching the Old Testament. That way, the theory went, my students would feel the full brunt of the old ache—the weight of sin and the hunger for salvation. When I got around to teaching Jesus, the good news would feel that much better.

Well, I can't do that. Never mind that it's bad theology—the good news is just too good! I'm not able to keep such a secret. How could I possibly know the full song begun in the Old Testament and not sing it out every time I teach? It's too explosive. If I tried to hold it in, I would burst.

QUESTIONS YOU MIGHT BE ASKING

All the study and reading you recommend won't fit into my week. How can I teach like you say when I don't have that much prep time?

I know it can be hard to devote the time. I'm often tempted to take shortcuts too. But remember, I refuse to treat you as if you don't care enough to take the time required to teach well. Good teaching *does* require quality prep time. So I challenge you to approach your teaching like the important work it is. We find time for what matters.

I can't tell Bible stories the way you do. Will your ideas still work for me?

I certainly hope so. Since I'm using personal examples in this book, most of them involve storytelling mixed with discussion. That's my style. Other teachers have other styles that work best for them. Some teach by leading a Bible study. Some lecture. Some use games or play. So I don't suggest you try to copy my style. Yet I hope that among the ideas I've shared, you'll find some you can fit to your style.

You mentioned three methods for getting to Jesus from an Old Testament passage: (1) what God does, (2) who God is, and (3) Jesus solves problems. Are there others?

In passing, I also mentioned prophecies about Jesus, types of Jesus, possible appearances of Jesus in the Old Testament, and passages in the New Testament that explain Old Testament stories in Jesus terms. So that's seven different ways, and we could add more.[2] I've recommended the methods I find easiest and most useful in teaching kids.

Does the age of the kids make a difference in how I teach the good news from the Old Testament?

Absolutely. Preschoolers are still learning the basic pieces of the whole Bible story, such as who God is and major characters and events. Sometimes I'm content to tell an Old Testament story in a God-centered way and leave it at that without connecting it to Jesus. That's still in the good-news spirit, and they'll put the pieces together later. But elementary kids should be learning how Old Testament stories fit into the larger good news, which means including Jesus. And older kids and teens especially need to be challenged to take the good news they've learned and consider how it should change the way they live. For example, in teaching the Balaam story to teens, I'd be sure to discuss how believing that Jesus takes evil meant to harm us and turns it to good makes a difference when people hurt us.

Your method makes it sound like the Old Testament only points ahead to Jesus. Wasn't he already working in Old Testament times too?

You're right—it's both. Already in the Old Testament the Son of God, who with the Father and the Spirit is eternal, was active in the world. He was creating, shepherding, defending his people, destroying evil—doing what God does. "He upholds the universe by the word of his power" (Hebrews 1:3). Likewise, in the Old Testament, God's people lived by faith, trusting his mercy even though Christ's saving work remained incomplete and shadowy. "For they drank from the spiritual Rock that followed them, and the Rock was Christ" (1 Corinthians 10:4). So in addition to pointing ahead to Jesus, the Old Testament also tells about his preincarnate work. This is one reason I don't discard the main point of an Old Testament passage even as I look beyond it. The moment we ask, "What is God doing in this story?" we're already opening our eyes to Jesus. He's there.

Show Them Jesus Right Away

Here are some ideas that will point kids to Jesus from the Old Testament, using what you've learned in this chapter. Use one or more of the following that fits your situation:

Teachers: The next time you prep an Old Testament lesson, use one of my three sets of questions as your method for connecting the passage to Jesus. The first method is often the easiest and works well with most stories.

- What is *God* doing for his people in this story?
- Good news! How does God do the same for us—only better—in Jesus?
- Believe it! How does believing this good news change how we live?

After a few lessons try the who-God-is and Jesus-solves-problems models as well. Always teach what you've noticed about Jesus as part of your lesson.

Preschool teachers: Come up with a teaching aid—such as the sign saying "Jesus"—to help turn attention to Jesus while telling Old Testament stories. Be creative. If you don't like the sign idea, use a handheld cross, or have your class chant a simple tune. Whatever you decide, use it as part of your class routine, being intentional about showing that the story isn't complete until you've included Jesus. Not only does this help your students get used to seeing Jesus in all parts of the Bible, but it will force *you* to remember to always include him.

Parents: Do you read through the actual Old Testament Bible story passages with your kids? If not, consider making it a bedtime ritual or a part of mealtime (so that you're feeding on God's Word too). One advantage of reading *through* the Old Testament story by story is that you learn the context of each passage as you go, which eliminates the need to spend much time studying beforehand. Each day just read the next passage and then discuss it using the questions suggested in this chapter. Let the whole family share (1) what they notice about God's work, his character, or a tension that needs to be resolved; (2) how this is expressed or solved in Jesus; and (3) how we'll live when we believe it.

If your church offers classes where the whole family learns about Jesus together, attend one with your kids. The chief way kids learn is by observing and copying you, so discovering Jesus *together* is one of the best ways you can teach them. If your church doesn't offer such classes, respectfully suggest it or offer to help organize one, either as an ongoing class or special event. If you're a ministry director, make a family class happen.

Anyone: Pick a New Testament book you're *not* teaching from and read it through—just to become more familiar with the good news of Jesus. Here's my promise: You'll end up discovering something that applies to a part of the Bible you *are* teaching. And it'll probably happen soon—within the next few times you teach.

Chapter 7
The Longest List in Church

Teaching the good news from the New Testament

The Captain's ruddy banner lifted high,
Makes hell retire and all the furies fly.
Yea, of his glory every recent glance
Makes sin decay and holiness advance.
—Ralph Erskine1

It was a few weeks into the Sunday school year, and the Bible story I was teaching was familiar. It was the one where Martha invited Jesus to her home and was busy preparing the meal while her sister Mary sat at Jesus's feet listening to his teaching. My students were older elementary church kids, so they'd heard it before.

I was determined to make *my* version of the lesson memorable and meaningful. I would go deep. With the characters in place—Martha in the kitchen and Mary sitting with Jesus—we picked up the story from Luke.

> Martha was distracted with much serving. And she went up to him and said, "Lord, do you not care that my sister has left me to serve alone? Tell her then to help me." But the Lord answered her, "Martha, Martha, you are anxious and troubled about many things, but one thing is necessary. Mary has chosen the good portion, which will not be taken away from her." (Luke 10:40–42)

I started with the obvious—comparing Martha with Mary. Mary makes an excellent example. To sit at the feet of a rabbi meant both learning from him and devoting one's life to following him. "But what about Martha?" I asked. "What do you think of what she did for Jesus?"

Some kids noticed that inviting Jesus to dinner and cooking for him was good. Others pointed out that it's only good if you have the right attitude. I agreed that Martha had some attitude problems. First, she got distracted. Jesus himself was visiting, but her attention was on dinner. Her work *for* Jesus had become more important to her than Jesus himself. Second, she wasn't really doing all that work for *Jesus*. She was actually doing it for herself—to get approval. We can tell because of how she got snippy when her efforts went unnoticed.

I talked about how easily we fall into the same trap. We act like we're serving Jesus, but we demand to be noticed. We say we love him but don't spend time with him. We forget that life with Jesus isn't first about what *we* do for *him*—it's about Jesus himself and how he's our Savior. "*That's* the good news," I said.

I reminded the kids that Jesus is better than anything else they might want. Better than achievements. Better than recognition. Far better than dinner. They all nodded in agreement. Of course. What kid is going to disagree when his Sunday school teacher is raving about how Jesus is better?

I decided to press them further, and I asked one more question: "*Why* is Jesus better?"

Three hands shot up. They knew the answer to this one. I called on one boy. "Because if we believe in him, we can go to heaven," he answered. The other two hands went down.

"Good!" I said. "What else?" No hands. "Brandon, you had your hand up," I said. "What were you going to say?"

"The same thing. I was going to say he takes us to heaven."

"Me too," said the third kid.

"Okay," I said. "But let's list some other things Jesus does for us. Tell me some." The kids just stared at me—annoyed. They'd answered my question the way it was always answered. They didn't see why they should have to think of anything else.

I had a problem.

A Puny Jesus

I had a group of church kids who could think of only one reason why Jesus is better than anything else. They were only using him to get to heaven. How could they ever love him that way? And why was their view of him so puny?

It couldn't *all* be my fault. Part of the problem, surely, was the Christian culture those kids were growing up in. It gave them a one-sided view of salvation. Once they'd made the decision of "believing in Jesus," the Christian life was about being good, and about choosing events or devotional habits that would help one feel spiritual. Jesus was left behind.

Still, I knew much of the fault *was* mine. In the few weeks I'd been teaching those kids, I too had glossed over the richness of salvation. I'd mentioned the good news, but it was stale. Each week I'd worked my way to some generic line about how Jesus is our Savior, but my "deep" lessons went no further. I hadn't dug up the details of all Jesus rescues us from, nor had I taught how he gives us hope, joy, forgiveness, holiness, peace with God, sonship, access to the Father, willing obedience—or any of the other gazillion blessings that are ours in Christ.

I'd failed in another way too. The Jesus I'd presented in my lessons was shallow. He did miracles and spouted wise sayings, but as a person I'd made him look about as interesting as one of those old flannelgraph cutouts. I'd failed to be fascinated by his character. The curriculum that year was all New Testament lessons. The full, explosive wonders of the good news were on display—Jesus was here! Yet, somehow, I was missing most of it.

The Mary and Martha lesson was one example. I'd made some points that deserved to be made about Martha's heart and how life with Jesus works, but that was all. I'd mostly missed Jesus—both the context of his work in the rest of Luke and his person as a character in the story.

I was railing against Martha but had actually done the same thing she did. I ignored Jesus.

THE CLASSROOM WALL

The next week I came to class with a plan. I had a sign that I taped to the wall. It read:

Jesus is better than anything else because...

"Here's what we're going to do," I told the kids. "Every week, when we're done with our lesson, we'll write out at least one thing we learned about Jesus that completes this sentence. Some weeks we may learn two or three things, or even five or ten things. But whatever we learn about Jesus we'll write down on a card and tape to this wall. We're making a list. This way I'll have to teach you about Jesus every week, and you'll learn lots of ways he's the best."

I laid out the rules: "Every card needs to be different—something new every week. And it has to be something amazing enough to go on the wall. We're going to do this all year."

One kid was looking at the wall, imagining. "That's going to be a long list," he said. "The longest list in church."

Exactly.

TWO THINGS TO REMEMBER

When teaching the good news from the New Testament, I remind myself to do the two things I forgot in that Mary and Martha lesson:

1. Look at the *work* of Jesus. This often means noticing the larger context of the passage I'm teaching.
2. Look at the *person* of Jesus. This usually means noticing details I might be used to skimming past.

This also means breaking old habits. Say I'm teaching about Jesus feeding the five thousand. Well, there's a boy in that story who shares his lunch. Kids relate to kids, and this kid shares. Great lesson on sharing, right?

But a glance at the context of this story shows that Jesus didn't use that incident to teach about sharing. He used it to teach about his saving work: "The bread that I will give for the life of the world is my flesh" (John 6:51).

A close reading of the story itself also makes Jesus come alive as a person. He's compassionate toward the crowd, despite being tired and grieving over his cousin's murder. He's concerned for the people's most basic needs. He's a man of action. He's thankful, practical, thrifty, and all-powerful. And through it all, he slyly manages to teach his disciples a lesson in faith. He's *interesting*—far more interesting than the boy—and worthy of worship.

The work and person of Jesus are connected, of course. But it helps to consider them separately.

THE WORK OF JESUS

Jesus's saving work is right in front of us in the New Testament. We don't have to take the story forward, as we did with the Old Testament. Yet we still might miss this good news if we read passages with narrow vision, blind to what's going on around them.

Are you teaching from the Gospels? Their theme is the person and saving work of Jesus. Is your lesson from Acts? That book is about the spread of this good news. The Epistles? All but a few of the short ones make the benefits of salvation a major topic. Revelation? It celebrates the completion of Jesus's work and his victory. There's only one way we could *possibly* teach from these books and miss the good news—and that's if we cut them into small sections, each a chapter or less, and taught each piece as if the rest did not exist.

Sound familiar?

That method is, of course, the typical approach to lessons for kids. We need to move beyond it. It takes a new mindset. Think of your lesson as part of a larger lesson contained in the whole book.

Example: The Work of Jesus in the Mary and Martha Story

Consider my Mary and Martha lesson. The book of Luke has a storyline. Early on, Luke speaks of Jesus being a Redeemer (Luke 1:68) and Savior (Luke 2:11). Then, about halfway through, Jesus begins talking about his coming death and resurrection, and he starts traveling to Jerusalem to die. That's where the visit with Mary and Martha happens—as Jesus and his disciples are "on their way" (Luke 10:38) to Jerusalem.

This makes the incident with Martha come alive. Look what Jesus lovingly taught her: Don't try to serve me; let me first serve you. Don't try to impress me; rely on me. Don't be anxious about pleasing me; just come to me.

On the way to the cross, that lesson fits. The cross is where Jesus frees us from the crushing, impossible pressure of having to serve God well enough. He rescues us from a worried-about-ourselves, Martha kind of relationship with God. In him we lay down our bowls, spoons, and every other burden—and enjoy divine fellowship.

How about that? A reason why Jesus is better than anything else.

Example: The Work of Jesus in the Good Samaritan Story

Think how we might teach the parable of the Good Samaritan in the larger context of Jesus's work. By itself, this parable easily makes kids feel insecure because the love shown by the Samaritan is extraordinary. Samaritans and Jews hated each other, but the Samaritan helps a dying Jew—a guy who might normally spit on him. The Samaritan risks his own life to help in every way possible—bandages, oil, wine, a ride, and payment for long-term care.

Jesus concludes by saying, "You go, and do likewise" (Luke 10:37). Gulp. Every time I've taught this lesson, kids have told me it sounds too hard—impossible.

So let's look at the context. The parable's setup is a talk between Jesus and a Jewish scholar. They establish that God's law is strict. It includes loving your neighbor as yourself. To make it doable, the scholar asks Jesus, "And who is my neighbor?" (Luke 10:29) He's hoping for a short list.

Ah. The scholar had the same concern my students have. The rule seems too hard. He expects Jesus to say something that lets him off the hook. That's the context. It means the Good Samaritan parable isn't just about helping hurt people; it's also about how to deal with the fact that God's commands seem impossible to keep.

Jesus's story defines "neighbor" in the broadest way possible. Relaxing the law isn't the answer. Instead, the parable gives another, better answer. Look how Jesus assigns the story's characters. If he was only trying to say "Love your enemy," he should have made the hurt guy a Samaritan and the helper a Jew—an example his Jewish listeners could relate to. But he made the hurt guy the Jew. While Jesus's command says, "Love your enemy," his story says, "Your enemy loved you."

This solves the problem both the scholar and my students struggle with. If you'd been saved from death and spectacularly loved by your enemy like in the story—well, then it becomes easier to *go and do likewise*, doesn't it? You actually might love an enemy in return. You could love that much because someone loved you that much.

I suspect the scholar remained puzzled. When had any Samaritan actually loved him? It was just a story. But whenever I get to this point in the Good Samaritan lesson, I tell kids *they* should understand, and those who know the rest of the Bible get it. The larger context—the rest of Luke and the entire Bible—tells us that "while we were enemies we were reconciled to God by the death of his Son" (Romans 5:10). Jesus loved us with an even more sacrificial love than the Samaritan. He not only risked his life but *gave* it.

God's rules are strict, yes. Jesus calls us to an extraordinary level of love that reflects his own love. But along with the instruction, he also shows us *how* to obey—through faith, depending on him, always deeply aware of how much he loved us first. *That* is how believers pursue God's commands.

The saving work of Jesus is all through the Good Samaritan story. Jesus provides the answer to the guilty, why-even-try reaction my students always have. Our failure is forgiven, and we're stirred to love our neighbors—even our enemies—as ourselves.

Example: The Work of Jesus in "Children, Obey Your Parents"

The Epistles are another place where we might miss the good news unless we notice the whole message of the book we're studying. Suppose we're teaching the popular verse, "Children, obey your parents in the Lord, for this is right" (Ephesians 6:1). That's a good lesson. Godly behavior is part of being joined to Jesus, so a lesson about obedience is connected to the good news—or it should be. The trick to *keep it connected* is to include the context.

First, notice the immediate context. The instruction to kids comes in the middle of a section about submission and love within relationships. Wives submit and husbands love. Children obey, and fathers be gentle. Slaves obey, and masters be kind. The basis for all these is found in Jesus: "the church submits to Christ" (Ephesians 5:24) and "Christ loved the church" (Ephesians 5:25).

Second, get a view for the whole book. Ephesians begins with a rundown of the many blessings we have in Christ. This is the basis for love and submission. The book ends with the famous instruction to put on God's armor—including salvation, the word of God, and prayer. From all this we get some possible teaching points:

- *Obedience is not for losers but for winners.* Jesus submitted and obeyed most fully of all, and his followers—including kids like you—do the same. It's a noble, exciting part of God's work in you.
- *Your obedience flows from what Jesus does for you.* When you obey, be encouraged. It shows he's working in you and loves you.

- *When you struggle to obey, you're not alone.* God fights with you and provides armor. Consider your salvation, believe his word, and pray to him. He will help you to obey.

All those points include the good news, and they come from the passage. We just have to see that the passage is bigger than a few verses.

THE *PERSON* OF JESUS

The second key to New Testament teaching is to notice the *person* of Jesus. Kids can't fully grasp the good news unless they see the whole, marvelous person at the center of it. It's normal for kids first to care about what Jesus gives them, but as they're drawn to him, they should also see his beauty. They must come to love the man himself.

The first point of studying the person of Jesus must always be to *wonder* at him, not to *copy* him. There are teachers who show kids how astounding Jesus is only to tell them, "You should be like that." Ouch! Those kids quickly get to where the last thing they want is to hear another way that Jesus is better. They learn to *resent* Jesus. Then our chance to wow them with Jesus is lost.

Yes, Jesus is our example. As kids come to love him, they will want to be like him. But first they need to be wonder-struck by him. When that happens regularly, wanting to be like him will follow naturally enough.

Example: The Person of Jesus in the Mary and Martha Story

The trick to noticing the person of Jesus is to *slow down*. In my Mary and Martha lesson I spent lots of time on Martha. She's a good character to learn from, but I should have also considered how the story revealed the main character—Jesus.

For starters, look how Jesus includes Mary. Rabbis in those days wouldn't teach women. It was demeaning. But Jesus has no concern for his reputation. He welcomes her at his feet, and then he defends her right to be there: "Mary has chosen the good portion, which will not be taken away from her" (Luke 10:42). Mary must be thrilled to hear that. She *is* in the right place. Jesus is not intimidated by Martha, and he won't abandon Mary—not for the sake of anyone, not ever.

There's more. Martha's complaint includes a swipe at Jesus: "Lord, do you not care that my sister has left me to serve alone?" (Luke 10:40). Well, he *does* care about both sisters—more than they know. Martha's accusation is horribly untrue. But unlike anyone I've ever met, Jesus feels no need to set the record straight. There's no bristling. No defensiveness. He lets all that self-concern go, thinking only of the sisters.

Jesus has audacious self-confidence without being at all self-important. He plainly claims his teaching matters more than Martha's cooking. He says it's the *one thing* that's necessary. If that came from anyone else, we would say, "What nerve!" But Jesus is so focused on others that he clearly isn't pompous. There is not a hint of boasting, yet no self-doubt either. That's unheard of.

Still more amazing is his gentle response to Martha's grumbling—"Martha, Martha" (Luke 10:41). His use of the double name is intimate. She's sinned against him, but this in no way lessens his resolve to love her. He doesn't get angry or annoyed or impatient—none of the things we wrongly imagine Jesus must feel toward us when we sin. None of that! Instead, he comes close. He corrects and restores. Martha's sin cannot separate her from Jesus's kindness.

All the time she was busy cooking, what Martha wanted was to be appreciated. She longed to be noticed by Jesus. It's every soul's need. Martha thought she was being ignored, but it turns out that Jesus was looking straight through to her heart. He'd noticed her all along—her anxiety and worry and even her sin. And he loved her still.

Now do you see why my lesson wasn't good enough? I missed an opportunity to teach *that*!

Tip for Seeing the Person of Jesus: Read and Observe

You may wonder where I eventually got these insights about Jesus and Mary and Martha. I got them from the Bible. I looked at the passage, and I spent about a half hour noticing details. Nothing more.

You can do this with any Gospel story. Simple observation is my favorite way to come up with rich material to teach about the person of Jesus. I highly recommend it.

My method is first to read the Bible story and its context. Then, with my Bible still open, I set aside thirty minutes and grab a notebook. I pick out a few key verses, or a central incident involving Jesus. Focused on just those few verses, I start making a list, writing down everything I notice that those verses reveal about the person of Jesus. Some things are obvious; I write them down anyway. Others take longer to notice, but as they come to me, I add them to the list.

After about ten or fifteen minutes I usually feel like I've thought of absolutely everything possible. I'm ready to quit. But the trick is to press on. Fill up a page or more. Keep thinking and writing for the full thirty minutes. Most often my best insights come near the end—after I'd thought I had nothing left to learn. That's when I might notice how Jesus does things in an order I wouldn't expect, or how he combines two or more virtues we almost never see together in anyone else.

I've done this for years and have never, *ever* found this to be a waste of time. There have been plenty of times I skipped it because I was lazy and told myself I didn't need it, but every time I've actually done it, it's paid off. Let's try one together.

Example: The Person of Jesus in the Healing of a Leper

The Gospel of Luke contains a brief account in which Jesus heals a leper. Full-blown leprosy in Jesus's day was painful and incurable. The diseased skin left lepers disfigured and smelly. It made them religiously impure, which—along with being contagious—got them labeled "unclean." They weren't allowed to come into towns or approach people. Unless a priest pronounced them well again, they were outcasts until they died. Here's Luke's account:

> While he was in one of the cities, there came a man full of leprosy. And when he saw Jesus, he fell on his face and begged him, "Lord, if you will, you can make me clean." And Jesus stretched

out his hand and touched him, saying, "I will; be clean." And immediately the leprosy left him. And he charged him to tell no one, but "go and show yourself to the priest, and make an offering for your cleansing, as Moses commanded" (Luke 5:12–14).

I recently taught this story for chapel time at a Christian school, and I began my lesson prep with a half hour of observation using these three verses. The list of things I noticed about Jesus filled two notebook pages. It's not particularly orderly, but here is my list:

» Jesus *touched him*, despite nasty leprosy.

» Sees that the guy needs tenderness as well as healing (probably hadn't been touched in ages).

» Healing is personal, not mechanical.

» *Reached out his hand* to touch the leper—doesn't recoil or take a step back, but moves toward the guy.

» Not afraid.

» Not repulsed.

» Drawn *to* what's nasty. Drawn *to* what I would run *from*.

» Doesn't scold the leper for coming into town and approaching—not even the slightest correction like, "You know, you shouldn't be here, but . . . ." Does Jesus not care about the rules?

» Jesus *does* care about the rules—sent leper to the priest.

» But the highest rule for Jesus is *faith*—responds when leper asks for help.

» Affirms that coming and asking of Jesus is right to do.

» His passion is to heal.

» Says, "I will"—what encouraging words! He *will* help those who come to him.

» What *power*! Cleanses full case of leprosy.

» Immediately! We might expect disease to end, but the effects— the unclean sores—take time to heal. But Jesus makes him totally clean immediately, sore-free, ready to see the priest.

» No doctor can do that, only Jesus.

» Jesus is not worried about becoming unclean.

» With anyone else, what's dirty contaminates what was clean. But it's the opposite with Jesus. His cleanliness makes the unclean clean.

» Says, "Be clean." Those are the words we all need to hear as people defiled by sin, and Jesus is happy to speak them.

» Heals quietly with a word—not *showy* despite being in town with people around.

» "Tell no one." Not concerned for fame.

» Leper says, "If you will, you can . . . ." Jesus is both *willing* and *able*—the combo we all need in a Savior.

» Leper is *full* of leprosy, but there's no sense from Jesus that this is an especially hard or unpleasant case.

» Jesus accepts, loves, fixes even the worst cases.

» Mix of *power* and *compassion* is stunning! How can a guy so powerful also be so tender and personal?

» Not aloof—wades right in and touches the most hideous guy in town.

» Could've healed with a word, but adds the touch.

» Why not heal first, then touch? The leper would still get touched. But Jesus touches us *in* our misery. He's not just tender to those who are doing better, but tender *in the midst* of our worst repulsiveness.

» Has a heart for outcasts.

» I'd feel for the leper emotionally, but stay back physically. Jesus goes to him with his *whole person*—soul and body.

» If Jesus had to reach out, the leper must have left some gap when he came up—but Jesus crosses it.

» The leper surely felt unfit to come all the way to Jesus, but Jesus goes all the way to him.

From this list, I picked three points to teach. I'll let you guess which ones they were. It hardly matters because there are easily a dozen strong ones. The true core of Jesus's beauty lies not in any one type of goodness but in the way such a phenomenal array of perfections comes together in one guy.

The leper's healing is surface-level Jesus. There are still deeper moments of his life—like when Jesus washes the disciples' feet or greets them after his resurrection. Look closely at those accounts, and you'll be dazzled. Do it lesson after lesson, and you'll start to see patterns. You'll feel the drumbeat of Jesus's life, and find yourself in step with the Holy One.

THE LONGEST LIST IS STILL GOING

So what happened with the longest list in church, from the beginning of this chapter? That year we ended up with seventy-four cards on the wall. The kids did some checking and found it was more than the books of the Bible but somewhat less than the names in the church phone directory—so it was not quite the longest list in the building, but close. The only thing that stopped us from making it longer was the end of the Sunday school year. It worked so well that the next year

I started a new list, and another the year after that—and every year since. Even when I'm teaching Old Testament lessons, I make sure that each week I teach at least one reason why Jesus is better than anything else.

Some cards repeat from year to year. But I also keep seeing new things about Jesus I never noticed before. The full list is still growing.

The kids enjoy it and I need it. It keeps me on track. When my teaching gets stale, the list forces me to remember that going deep with a lesson includes looking deeply at Jesus. "For what we proclaim is not ourselves, but Jesus Christ as Lord" (2 Corinthians 4:5).

Why the List Matters

There's another, more important reason why I need "the longest list": you and I and the kids we teach need the person and work of Jesus always set in front of us—right before our eyes.

Consider what it means to have such a stunning Savior. First, joined to him we are counted as righteous as the marvelous person he is. We have power to live like he did, and we look forward to living that way perfectly one day. The list fills us with confidence and expectation about ourselves.

Second, Jesus is the reigning King and coming Judge. We might fear the Judge—but look what kind of guy he is! His compassion and tenderness toward believing sinners is all over the longest list. The Judge is a friend of believers. He wants us to look to him *in our struggles*, not just when we have our act together. So why stay distant? Why pray timidly or be nervous about judgment? Do you see? The longest list helps us trust our Lord.

Finally, this person—this Jesus—is God. Many kids misunderstand God. They know he's supposed to be loving and helpful. They also know he's supreme and powerful, requiring worship and obedience. All that sounds troubling—like God is moody, or bossy, or claims to care but has a dark side. They aren't eager to worship him. They aren't even sure they *like* him.

But what if Jesus is right when he says, "Whoever has seen me has seen the Father" (John 14:9)? Could it be true that if we look at what Jesus is like, we see what God is like?

Think about Jesus. He isn't anything like the moody, distant God many kids imagine. In Jesus, God's absolute authority and his utter love come together—and the result is "Wow!" In lesson after lesson kids need to see a thousand wonder-filled details that make up the character of Jesus, until they realize, with a gasp, that they have seen the face of God. And God is so, so good.

At that point, the idea that God has a dark side crumbles. Never again will they fall for any lesser view of God. They know better—because they know Jesus.

QUESTIONS YOU MIGHT BE ASKING

It sounds like your list about Jesus is full of comforting stuff like his kindness. What about the places where he speaks of judgment and warns about hell and such? Do you teach that too?

I do, and those things make the list of ways Jesus is better. The Heidelberg Catechism teaches that judgment of unbelief is a good thing and a comfort for believers. It assures us that Jesus's enemies, and ours, will be defeated: "In all my distress and persecution I turn my eyes to the heavens and confidently await as judge the very One who has already stood trial in my place before God and so has removed the whole curse from me."[2]

Warnings too are part of Jesus's kindness and care. The fact that this talk of judgment comes from a person we know to be self-sacrificing and humble—one who has taken for us the curse he warns of—ought to encourage us. Jesus does not switch willy-nilly between being an angry, scolding person and a kind, patient one. When he gets harsh with people, it always stems from their unbelief. Struggling sinners who believe find him softhearted. This should stir us all the more to throw all our trust onto him.

Do you really need that much context—like the whole book—when you're going to teach one Bible passage? It sounds like a lot of reading.

Yes, I read that much. I didn't used to, but by doing it I've come to enjoy it. I learn a lot that way. And I put it to you that if you're going to teach from the Bible, you ought to read the Bible—beyond a few verses. It's good for your own spiritual growth as well, which is essential if you hope to help kids grow.

You seem to come up with a lot of points to teach in every lesson. Shouldn't you keep it simpler?

Yes, I'm guilty. I often try to teach too much at one time. Please don't think you have to do it all in every lesson. Especially with younger kids, it's probably best to teach just one aspect of Jesus's work one week and then an aspect of his person the next. I'd do well to take my own advice in this regard.

Show Them Jesus Right Away

Now you're ready to make Jesus come alive for your kids when teaching from the New Testament. Consider using one or more of these ideas.

Teachers: Start a "longest list" for your class. Write "Jesus is better (than anything else) because..." and post it where you meet, in a place that's noticeable. Then each time you teach, add a new way to complete that statement. For example, a lesson on the healing of the leper might mean adding a card that says, "He has power to heal *anything* that's wrong with me," or "He's kind to hurting, despised people"—or both! I usually pick what goes on the cards because it helps me keep my lesson focused. However, you could also discuss the lesson with your class and let *them* write something they learned about Jesus, especially if you're a youth leader or teacher for older kids. Make sure it's something new every time so that you're forced to look deeply at Jesus and discover things about him you hadn't noticed before.

Preschool teachers: One way to keep a "longest list" for non-readers is to use a voice recorder. When you start the list, record your whole class saying together "Jesus is better because . . . ." Then, with each lesson you teach, add one thing you learned about Jesus to your recording. Little kids love to hear their own recorded voices played back to them; they'll surely ask to hear the entire recording often. Each time you play it for them, you'll be reviewing past lessons—and teaching them that Jesus is better than anything else in *so many* ways.

Parents: A good home version of the "longest list" is to make a poster in the room where you have family devotions or read the Bible to your kids. Write the heading "Jesus is…" on the poster. Then as you read or study a gospel or epistle together, pick a new way to complete the sentence in a word or two. Add those words to your poster, or let younger kids draw pictures to represent what they learned about Jesus. Adding just a few words to a poster each time lets you do the exercise daily without covering your house in writing—and, of course, keeps your kids paying attention to the Bible and to Jesus.

Anyone: If it's been a while (or never) since you've read straight through a gospel, set aside an hour—it'll take two at the most—and read the book of Mark in a single sitting. By reading it straight through, you'll see themes and directions in Jesus's life that you might have otherwise missed. Read it *as a story*, not a study. You'll appreciate Jesus in new ways as a person and better understand the context of his work. I have little doubt that what you notice from your reading will pop up in your teaching sometime soon.

Chapter 8

The Grapes That Taught Good News

Taking the good news beyond lesson time

Let such as have received great things from God maintain
a certain greatness of spirit suitable to their interest in him.
I do not mean a haughty spirit, swelled with pride,
for that is altogether unsuitable to a saving interest in God,
"who beholds the proud afar off"; but a humble spirit greatened
by continual converse with the great God; who by raising up
His servants' hearts to the contemplation and fruition
of higher objects, maketh them too big for this world.
—John Arrowsmith[1]

People sometimes ask how I decided to write this book. I tell them it started with grapes.

This chapter is about creating an atmosphere in our classrooms, youth groups, clubs, and camps that fits the good news. Much of this will carry over into home life too, but I especially want to speak to you in terms of your role in "organized ministry"—whether you're a parent, a humble assistant, or a ministry director. We all contribute to an atmosphere, and we need to remember the old adage that kids learn more from what we do than from what we say—and that they learn more from what we say in our unplanned, unscripted moments than from our prepared lessons. I didn't start thinking hard about what it means to be a good-news teacher until I began considering this.

A Class with a Problem

The eye-opener came with a brand new class. I'd taken a job that required moving across the country. My family found a church in our new town, and we settled in. It didn't take long before our new church was looking for volunteers to teach kids for the upcoming school year. I was happy to be approved and assigned to teach fourth-grade Sunday school.

The ministry director went over things with me—curriculum, schedule, safety procedures. She also handed me a tall stack of play money—"Bible Bucks," the currency read. It looked like it'd been printed on the church copy machine and cut on the big paper cutter in her office. The Bible Bucks were for me to hand out as incentives in class. I could award them however I liked—for attendance, learning Bible verses, right answers, good behavior, whatever. Twice a year the Sunday school ran a store where kids could spend their bucks on candy and toys. She could get me more if I needed them, she said.

Okay, I thought. I didn't usually teach that way, but it wasn't the first time I'd seen a kids' ministry that used a reward system. No reason to make a fuss; if the kids were used to it, I'd hand out bucks.

Then I taught my first class. I started by getting to know the kids. I asked them about school and family, and then let them ask me questions. They mostly wanted to know my policy on bucks. What should they do to earn a lot? Would I give more for memorizing a verse, or for participation during singing time?

Then I taught a lesson. One boy got upset when I didn't reward his good answer with bucks. We closed with a Bible memory game and—you guessed it—the kids all wanted to know how many bucks the winning team would get.

I stopped the game and looked at them. I thought for a moment. "None," I said.

Then and there I decided that the bucks had to go.

Changing the Tone

It wasn't just that the bucks were a distraction and an idol. The kids' attitudes also confirmed what my gut felt when I first heard about the bucks: a classroom culture built on rewards for performance wouldn't fit the good news I planned to teach.

It wouldn't do to teach that God's rewards in salvation come freely, by grace, but that rewards in the church come by being good and memorizing verses. Nor would it work to teach that God values faith over superior churchy behavior, and then give prizes to kids who excel in churchy behavior. I couldn't say that Jesus is better than absolutely anything else, but reward what kids learned about him with a slip of paper redeemable for candy.

All rewards aren't automatically wrong, but for those kids in that class, those bucks were working against the good news. I don't know how it got that way. That church had solid teaching. The ministry director was one of the best I've ever worked with and supported my decision to stop giving out bucks. The other children's workers and parents I knew all seemed to value the good news. But somewhere along the way the bucks had been introduced and a tone had been set. It had to change.

The Generous Vineyard Owner

I told the kids I wouldn't be handing out Bible Bucks for anything they did and explained why. God's greatest rewards are based on his generosity, not what we've earned. Our class would work the same way.

I still planned to give bucks, I told them. On store day everyone who came to class would get an envelope full of bucks to shop with. It'd be the same amount for all. It would not be earned. It would be a gift—like God's gifts.

"But what if someone who hardly ever comes to class shows up on store day?" they asked. "Then you'll give them, like, half as many bucks as the rest of us, right?"

"Nope," I said. "We'll share with them just as generously as if they'd been here every week. Everyone gets the same."

To help the point stick, the week before store day I taught Jesus's parable of the workers in the vineyard. A landowner goes out at daybreak to hire workers for his vineyard, promising to pay a normal day's wage. At midmorning he hires more workers and sends them to the vineyard too, promising to pay them what's fair. He does the same at noon, midafternoon, and an hour before quitting time.

I brought in several clusters of grapes to illustrate the story. We made five piles. There was a large pile of grapes to represent all the work done by the guys hired first, down to a pile that contained just one measly grape.

"Those last guys hardly did any work at all," I said, "but at the end of the day the owner paid them first and gave them a full day's pay."

I put one silver coin next to the single grape. Then I told how each of the other groups of workers in Jesus's story also got the same pay—one coin. Everyone received one day's pay, though the guys hired first weren't happy about it.

The kids and I had much to talk about. We ate grapes together while we discussed fairness and God's generosity. We talked about how incredibly generous God is to us, how he gave his Son, and how good it is that his gift to us is based on his generosity rather than what we've earned. We considered how this should make us humble, content, and eager to share.

"Now I understand about the bucks," one boy said. "It's like the grapes." They were ready for store day.

IS IT TRUE?

That week I got a call from the mom of a girl in my class. She told me her daughter had a friend who'd never been to church. They'd often invited her, and the friend's parents finally said yes. So her daughter would be bringing the friend to class the coming Sunday—on store day.

Mom was concerned. Once her daughter found out the friend could come, the daughter had started talking about the store. She'd told the friend everyone would get play money to shop with. Even the friend, as a visitor, would get just as much as the kids who came all year—or so her daughter claimed. Mom wanted to make sure it was true. It sounded like a misunderstanding. Might the friend end up disappointed? And what did it have to do with grapes?

I assured Mom that her daughter understood correctly. In my class the bucks were a gift, not a reward.

Sure enough, that Sunday the friend was in class. I didn't even have to explain about the store. The rest of the kids saw the visitor and started telling her, "We'll all get the same gift—even you." "It's because God is generous." "When we do it this way, it's like Jesus. You don't have to earn what you get from Jesus. You just believe."

It had taken half a year, but that class was changing. A good-news culture was growing.

CREATING A GOOD-NEWS ENVIRONMENT

I never saw that girl again, but I know she learned something memorable about Jesus. It wasn't directly due to anything I taught but because she entered a good-news environment that was different from the rest of the world.

Kids need that—church kids as much as visitors. The world teaches them that success comes from feeling good about themselves and being the best, and they bring that philosophy to church. They quickly move from being Christians to believing they have to be the *best* Christians. I see it all the time—kids who are nervous every time they pray in a group because their prayers might not sound good enough, or kids who learn Bible verses to show off. Where can these kids find a place where contentment springs from being joined to Jesus, not the approval of others? Where can they be freed from self?

It must happen when they walk into our classrooms, camps, clubs, and youth groups. They must enter a completely new universe—one with good-news sensibilities. Creating this universe is different for every bunch of kids, but some principles can guide us.

A good-news environment is sin-aware.

We don't pretend that kids are basically good and just need a little direction. Instead, we expect absolutely everyone (including ourselves) to arrive with big problems only Jesus can fix. We build up kids' confidence and give them comfort *in Christ*—by pointing them away from themselves and to the only perfect Holy One.

A good-news environment is grace-aware.

We celebrate and model the work of Christ for us and in us, and give God the credit for every good change that happens in a kid's life. We expect God to bring growth. This creates a place of mercy and openness because when God gets the credit for spiritual progress, there's no need for either one-upmanship or defensiveness, only deeper faith.

A good-news environment focuses on the heart.

We're never satisfied with manipulating outward behavior, but instead recognize that kids who look obedient still need Jesus—maybe more than kids who *aren't* obedient. We don't let either rule-keeping kids *or* rule-breaking kids use their behavior as a way to avoid Christ. We seek heart-level growth in both.

A good-news environment helps kids to find Jesus delightful.

We won't let kids use Jesus to get something else they want more. We don't approach teaching, prayer, and worship as things to be done because they're important and necessary—after which we turn to more "fun" activities when it's time to enjoy oneself. Rather, we communicate that *nothing is more enjoyable* than Jesus.

The Bible Bucks system violated every one of these principles. It overlooked the sin the bucks fed. It failed to model grace. It rewarded outward behavior rather than working on the heart. Worst of all, it assumed that the delightfulness of Jesus wasn't enough of a draw without some further incentive. That's why it had to change.

THE BEST PLACE TO BE CAUGHT IN SIN

One big way we set a tone is by how we deal with misbehavior. Simply telling kids to stop their bad behavior—along with, perhaps, a guilt-pressure comment that "Jesus doesn't like you to do that"—is seldom the best approach.

I was teaching a group of young teens several years ago when I noticed two girls glaring at each other. It turns out they'd had a fight a few days before and weren't over it. As my lesson went on, they started calling each other names. I told them to quit it, but a few minutes later they were at it again.

I wasn't about to have my lesson interrupted any further, so I sent them both out of our lesson circle. I told one girl to sit in one corner of the room and put the other girl in another corner. "If you have a fight, don't bring it in here," I told them. "We don't speak to each other like that. I expect you to behave *properly* here." I left them to think about it and went on teaching.

I had handled it horribly. Yes, I had to preserve order, and I was right to insist that our group be a safe place for everyone. But think about the messages I sent. I acted shocked that sin popped up in my classroom, and essentially sent the message that the group was the last place you wanted to be caught sinning. You needed to be extra good here.

Compare this to the woman in the Bible who was caught in adultery. The Pharisees suggested stoning her. Jesus said whoever was without sin should throw the first stone, and they all left. He forgave the woman and told her, "Go, and from now on sin no more" (John 8:11). For her, the *best* place to be caught in sin was next to Jesus. He could save her from condemnation and help her repent.

I could have done so much more for those girls. I had an assistant in the room. A helper who'll speak the good news to kids is invaluable. She could have taken those girls aside and talked with them, or I could have done it myself while the helper kept the rest of the group occupied. Maybe my prepared lesson wouldn't have been taught because I was busy with those girls. That would have been okay. The message that we deal with sin beats any prepared lesson anyway.

If a kid is going to get caught in sin, what better place than a class about Jesus—where there are people and tools that can help? Imagine if our group were the sort of place where it was safe to admit your sin. What if we had a habit of confessing our struggles and applying the good news? Maybe those girls would have come expecting help to get over their fight. Wouldn't that have been great?

How to Talk to a Sinner

Suppose I could go back and do it over again. I'd take time to listen to those girls and let them share their hurt. And then what? What could I say to each of them?

I could talk about her heart. I could ask what made her misbehave. It wasn't just the other girl's sin against her. It was also her own angry desire to be top dog and to hurt back—which came from fear of being put down or disliked.

I could talk about real forgiveness. I could let her know that I'm not looking for an outward fix just to get the class running smoothly again. There would be no forced, fake apologies. Instead, we'd work toward her and the other girl sincerely forgiving each other—if not right away, then someday soon. God makes us able to do that.

I could talk about Jesus. I could tell her how, in him, she's forgiven for hurting the other girl—and that he forgives the other girl for the ways she was hurtful too. I could tell her how Jesus fills her heart needs—and that the fear of being disliked can fade away as she enjoys his forgiveness and sees how much he delights in her. He loves her.

I could talk about who she is in Jesus. I could explain that she's not a bad kid because she was fighting—she's a child of God who behaved badly and needs to repent. Repenting is a happy, holy thing God's people do, and he makes her able. She *can* forgive the other girl. She can come to love that girl like Jesus loves—yes, that much!

I could pray with her. I could thank God that she's eternally forgiven and ask him to give her the desire and power to forgive the other girl.

I could show her grace. I could forgive her for disrupting my lesson and let her rejoin the group. Even if she isn't ready to fully forgive the other girl yet, she can take part as long as doing so won't further harm her or others.

Then, one more thing—a critical one: I could confess my own sin. I must model what I want her to practice by telling her how I sometimes get angry and hurt people too. I could give an appropriate example to make it a true confession rather than a vague admission. As part of my prayer with her, I might ask her to pray for me not to be angry as well. I do this because if the group is going to be a place where confession thrives and it's safe to seek help in Jesus—well, it has to start with me, the teacher.

I might even take the opportunity to confess in front of the whole group. A good-news environment requires the teacher to model repentance. Not every sin is appropriate to share with students, but they need to know some real and ugly sins I struggle with. They need to see how, in Jesus, I find forgiveness and the power to repent.

This helps the naughty kids deal with their misbehavior—but it's even more important for the teacher-pleasing kids who arrive trying to show how good they are. It tells them not to be proud or put their hope in their own goodness. It points all kinds of kids to the Savior.

Why I Fail

Now, all this is what I *wish* I'd do every time kids seriously misbehave. In reality, other duties and limited time get in my way. My desire to look good interferes too. Sometimes I prefer to put on a saintly image rather than talk about my sin, or I hesitate to discuss Jesus stuff with a kid who might scoff at it. I also find myself keeping order as my first priority and training hearts as a distant second—because a teacher who keeps order looks good to outsiders.

So I struggle. With most misbehavior cases I accomplish only a fraction of what I wish I would do. I mess up, get lazy, or chicken out. But I'm learning.

I recently had a nasty squabble break out between two boys during a group game. One accused the other of cheating. There were threats, tears, and hateful words. I stopped the game. I said I thought it was best to quit playing if the game was leading some of us to sin. That wasn't a scolding or a ploy to make anyone feel guilty; I just wanted us to be sin-aware. I pointed out that competitive games are fun but they sometimes bring out selfishness. I suggested that instead of playing the game, we all take a few minutes to pray that we wouldn't be selfish.

The amazing thing was they agreed. Those kids love game time, but there wasn't a single protest. Not even a disappointed sigh. I told them we had to stop playing, put away the game, and spend time praying instead—and they *liked* the idea. They knew it was the right thing to do. They expected it. This showed that God was at work in those kids, and I told them so.

But as I thought about it afterward, I realized it showed that God was working in me too. I'm starting to dare to act like a good-news teacher often enough that the kids are getting used to it—and copying it.

Good-News Encouragement

Of course, most of our kids' programs consist of more than just lessons. I want to address these other areas now, beginning with the little corrections and encouragements all of us can constantly give. We don't always have time to stop and ask deep questions, but we can still focus on the heart and guide kids to the cross.

The best opportunities often come when we might be thinking least about teaching the good news, such as during games or when we're serving food. Sin tends to show up during these activities, so for years I always passed out snacks with the instruction, "Remember to share." More recently I've changed that to, "Be careful; greed is dangerous." I think my new line sets a better tone. It's aware of the heart, not mere behavior. It fits people who know that sin runs deep but that God's people can resist it—even at the heart level.

Jesus taught like that. When a man asked him, "Teacher, tell my brother to divide the inheritance with me," Jesus's answer was, "Take care, and be on your guard against all covetousness" (Luke 12:13, 15). Then he told how the riches we have with God are worth more than the worldly things we get anxious over. Jesus aimed at hearts and pointed people to God. We must teach the same way.

God brings repentance in kids' hearts. And when he does, I try to remember to give him the credit.

The world's way is to give kids the credit. It builds self-esteem by congratulating them when they do well. That *sounds* encouraging, but praising kids when they're right is little different from scolding them when they're wrong. The focus is on their behavior, ignoring their faith in Jesus.

We shouldn't build self-esteem. We should build Christ-esteem. We must give kids the best kind of encouragement of all—the kind that comes from knowing that Jesus is in you and for you. When I see growth in a kid, I try to remember to tell him how much I see God at work in his life. Those little encouragements add up.

If you're a group leader, camp counselor, helper, or greeter—or have some other role that doesn't involve directly teaching Bible lessons—you still have enormous impact on kids. You probably have more informal time with them than the person teaching lessons does. Use that time. Make it rich with talk about Jesus.

GOOD-NEWS DISCUSSIONS

Many programs have discussion groups that are separate from lesson time. If you lead one of these, be sure to help kids connect the good news to their daily lives. Do the same if you're a parent asking your kid what class was about. When I'm stumped for a good question to ask,

I run through four basic categories—four ways the good news affects our daily behavior.

What the good news gives	Discussion questions
Gratitude	• What did we learn about Jesus that makes us thankful to him? • What opportunities will you have to show your thankfulness this week? How can you remember Jesus at those times?
Confidence	• What did we learn about how God empowers his people, making them able to serve and obey him? • What helps from the Spirit shall we use to become better servants of God? (Examples of help from the Spirit are prayer, the Bible, and support from others in the church.)
Hope	• What did we learn about why following Jesus is exciting and worth it? • What sometimes feels better than Jesus? Tell about times when putting him first seems to cost you too much. How can you believe Jesus is better at those times?
Comfort	• What did we learn that might make you scared you aren't good enough? Be glad you're forgiven in Jesus! • Which things do you avoid doing for God because you might fail? How might you be brave because you know God accepts you even when you fail?

Notice that you don't have to worry so much about telling kids what to do. You just recall the good news and the Bible lesson and let *it* provide the push. It's often best to let the students themselves tell you how they believe God needs to work in their lives.

GOOD-NEWS WORSHIP

Many programs also have a singing or worship time. Leaders in charge of this time have a huge opportunity to create a good-news atmosphere that will affect the entire program. Proper worship of God never strays far from the good news. It's inspired *by* it and praises God *for* it.

If you're a song leader, you teach by what you say and what you choose to sing. Remind kids of the good news as you introduce songs. Pick songs that praise God, rather than songs that mostly celebrate *us*. It's fine to sing about our feelings—the Psalms cover all sorts of emotions—but biblical worship connects our feelings to God's character and saving work. "Oh sing to the LORD a new song, for he has done marvelous things!" (Psalm 98:1).

It's frighteningly easy to pander to what creates a feel-good worship experience and make Jesus an afterthought. I've caught myself doing it. I've led kids in songs to get a mood going or to burn off energy. It may have worked, but in some cases neither I nor the songs even mentioned God. Youth groups, in particular, can easily become defined by their style of music. It's the fuel for the gathering and gives the group its identity.

I love good music, but our students need *Jesus* to be their identity. They're actually *yearning* for us to give them the good news.

I was reminded of this a few years ago when I was asked to lead a youth group in an hour-long prayer session. Praying together for a whole hour was new to those kids. They had trouble staying alert. So about halfway through I decided, on the spot, to throw in a song. "Let's take a break and *sing* a prayer," I told them.

I looked around. There was no praise band. No projection system. Not even a guitar. Maybe I'd spoken too quickly. But we were in a church sanctuary and there were hymnals. I grabbed one and found a prayerful hymn I knew. The words were old-fashioned but praised the person and work of Jesus with depth, so I called out the number. We passed around the songbooks and sang all five verses without accompaniment.

It sounded pretty bad to me. We were clunky and out of tune. But when we were done, as we bowed our heads to resume praying, I overheard one girl whisper to her neighbor, "That was cool. I've never sung from a hymnal before." *Cool?*

Maybe she liked the novelty. And young people often enjoy tradition above new styles. But I think the main reason that girl found singing from the hymnal "cool" was because the entertainment trappings she was used to had been stripped away. It was just a prayer to Jesus, beautifully written and humbly sung.

I'm always baffled when people say great music and an energetic leader, combined with fun games to create a high-energy event, will get kids excited about Jesus. Really? Those are all fine things, and I can see how they might get kids excited—about the music, about the leader, or about the games. But if we want them to get excited *about Jesus*, don't we have to make sure we show them Jesus?

GOOD NEWS OR GIMMICK?

Games and other fun activities are also a part of many programs, and these require care as well. When we tell ourselves we're using these things to draw kids into a group (so we can make much of the good news once they're in), that bait-and-switch sends a message.

Now, hear me correctly: Fun activities *do* fit life with Jesus. We're joyful people. Fun is good. And older kids, in particular, need social interaction with other kids and adults in the church. Add the need to welcome newcomers who aren't yet excited about Jesus, and you have good reasons to expand a church's ministry beyond simple classes. If you lead games, you'll have many informal opportunities to show the love of Christ and tell about him. That's great!

Yet I'm convinced it's unwise to use fun social events as the *primary* draw to get kids in the door of the overall ministry. We shouldn't let fun become a tool to keep kids interested so we can feed them some good news on the side. *Jesus isn't a side dish.*

If I can't get little ones excited about Sunday school without pretending we're jungle explorers or astronauts, or if I need carnival games to keep the youth group together, I've already lost. The subtle message of those gimmicks is that jungles and space stations and carnivals are more exciting than Jesus. If Jesus were more exciting, wouldn't *he* be the selling point?

156

Jesus didn't call people by saying, "Join me for a good time"—even though joining him was the best possible life to be had. Nor did he tell people they'd enjoy sweet camaraderie—though that too ended up being the best. Jesus called people to himself. He called them to discipleship and service in his kingdom. He proclaimed the good news and said, "Follow me."

What if we were up-front about Jesus being our highest delight? What if we first of all invited kids to encounter him and his good news—and as an outgrowth of all the joy and freedom Jesus gives us, we also had a lot of fun? What if as a result of serving a great Savior together, we built great relationships? The difference is subtle. But the message it sends changes the tone of the group.

We must believe there are kids in whom the Holy Spirit is working, and once they get a real taste of Christ, they will be irreversibly captured for his kingdom. Rather than pander to kids who are looking for a good time—even a churchy good time—we must offer life to kids who are thirsting for something the world can't provide.

The Grapes Teach Again

Back to our grapes. It's been several years since I thought I'd solved the problem of the Bible Bucks. In time the entire Sunday school program decided to give the bucks only as gifts rather than as rewards. To cut down on greed, we also decided to have store day just once a year, at Christmas. That makes it easy to encourage kids to buy gifts for others instead of just grabbing stuff for themselves.

I still teach about the grapes. I make it a special lesson each year, the week before the store. I make sure the kids understand that we don't earn God's approval by doing churchy things. Problem fixed. Right?

Wrong. This past year on store day, after all my instructions and explanations, as the kids were getting ready for me to hand out their bucks, I heard them talking to each other about what they planned to buy. They were bragging. They couldn't brag about how much they had to spend, since everyone had the same amount. Instead, they were talking about their generosity and comparing their goodness.

"I'm going to spend *all* my bucks on presents for my family."

"Are you going to get candy for yourself? You know, it's better to get presents for other people. That's what I'm doing."

One timid girl didn't join the chatter. Instead, she pulled me aside. She looked at me with a smile and whispered, "I'm going to spend all my bucks on presents for others too." I believed her. She truly has a generous heart and probably would have bought gifts even without pressure from the other kids. In fact, I came close to telling that sweet girl how good she was being and how proud I was of her—until something told me that's what she was after. She wanted my approval. All the bragging had made her want to get some credit too.

I looked her in the eye. I quietly told her, "You know I hope you won't be selfish at the store. But I don't want you to feel proud at the store either if you only buy presents. You can spend your bucks any way you want. I won't like you any more or less, and God won't either."

As soon as I said it I wondered if I'd gone too far. It might have sounded like generous behavior doesn't matter. But as I look back, I realize it was exactly what the situation called for. I had to be *that* radical about God's grace.

I called the whole group together. "Remember how we all get the same amount of bucks?" I asked. "It's because we don't earn points with God for how well we learn in class." They nodded. "Well, we don't earn points with God for being unselfish either. So let's be careful not to get proud about giving presents. God welcomes you as his child because Jesus is good, not because you're good enough to earn it. You don't have to prove to him or any of the rest of us how unselfish you are."

Then in the same classroom where I'd confronted greed years earlier, we now prayed together about self-righteous pride. We confessed that the store brought out sin. We asked God to help us shop without either being selfish *or* showing off. We prayed that no one would feel guilty for spending bucks on themselves, and we prayed that no one would feel better than others for buying presents. We prayed that our confidence would be in Jesus instead, no matter how we shopped.

You see, the good news *never* becomes old news. It *always* has more to teach. It keeps changing us, burrowing into the soul and rooting out deeper sins.

Then we went shopping. It was a good day.

QUESTIONS YOU MIGHT BE ASKING

Are rewards for spiritual behavior always bad? Wouldn't giving such rewards teach kids that we consider spiritual things important?

That thinking makes some sense. It's one reason rewards might *sometimes* be good, if done carefully. Creating a good-news environment takes knowing your students and how they tend to miss Jesus; different things work with different batches of kids. Still, I generally don't recommend rewards. Teaching kids that spiritual things are important might make them churchy, but I have a bigger goal. I want to teach them the good news, which tells us (1) the best rewards are not material but spiritual and (2) these are never earned or deserved by our religious behavior.

One test of any kids-ministry gimmick is to ask what we'd think if adult ministries used the same technique. What if adults got prizes for perfect attendance at church, memorizing Bible verses, or bringing a visitor to the service? Chances are we'd object. We wouldn't just say it was childish—we'd say God doesn't work that way. We're supposed to do these things out of love for him, not to get prizes.

You mentioned confessing your sins to your students. Are you sure that's wise?

It has to be appropriate confession. There are two things to watch out for: (1) The details of some sins aren't suitable to tell anyone but a few trusted confidantes, and many sins aren't right to tell kids or aren't appropriate for a teacher-student relationship. (2) Be careful not to get self-absorbed. We shouldn't anxiously look at ourselves. We should confidently look to Jesus.

If you watch out for those traps, honest confession powerfully communicates the good news. It says we have freedom to admit sin openly, without fear, because our hope is in Jesus rather than in our performance or appearance. And it says we're eager to forsake that sin and repent, openly and boldly—because of Jesus.

SHOW THEM JESUS RIGHT AWAY

There's something in this chapter for everyone—something *you* can put to use now. Pick something that applies to your role, and run with it.

Classroom workers: Make a checklist for yourself out of the four characteristics of a good-news environment, listed near the beginning of this chapter. It should look something like:

Sin-aware
- ☐ I acknowledged our struggle with sin (including my own).
- ☐ I built up kids' confidence *in Christ*, not in themselves.

Grace-aware
- ☐ I celebrated and modeled the freeness of all God gives.
- ☐ I gave credit *to God* (not to the kid) for growth I noticed in kids' lives.

Heart-focused
- ☐ I addressed heart attitudes rather than coercing outward behavior.
- ☐ I urged both rule-breakers and rule-keepers to trust Jesus rather than their behavior.

Delighted with Jesus
- ☐ I treated nothing as more enjoyable than Jesus.
- ☐ I valued connecting to Jesus through prayer, worship, and the Bible.

After each class, go through your checklist and grade yourself. Make it part of your post-class routine, so you constantly notice the environment you're creating and get better at making it fit the good news.

Parents: Use the above checklist for your home life. Look at it in the evening, and grade yourself on how you did with your kids that day. I need to add here that full-time parenting is a difficult spiritual chore. It'd be easy to look at your list each day and feel discouraged or condemned by your failure to live up to it, so as you go through it, *also turn to God.* Thank him that he—not you—is the determining factor in building faith in your children, and that he loves you and uses you despite your repeated failings. Ask him to help both you and your children delight more in Jesus.

Anyone: Test the tone of your time with kids by occasionally asking them this question: "What do you think I want most for you?" Their responses might disappoint you. As hard as you try to emphasize the good news, kids might still say that they think your chief goal is to get them to behave better, to give them Bible knowledge, or to be fun—as well as other unexpected answers. This will let you know what you need to change. Kids will retain only a fraction of what you tell them, so what sticks? Usually, it's whatever you're most excited about. Try to give Jesus first place.

Discussion leaders: Write down the discussion questions in this chapter that go with the four things the good news gives—gratitude, confidence, hope, and comfort. Most lessons fit one of those themes. If you keep those questions with you when you lead discussions, you'll usually have at least one ready question that draws on the good news.

Song leaders: Look through the songs you regularly lead. Which ones actually tell the good news? It may be helpful to make a written copy of the words and go through them, circling the best expressions of the gospel. This will help you remember those lines so you can point out those truths to kids the next time you lead those songs. If you find some songs that don't celebrate God or the good news, consider replacing them with songs that do.

Worship leaders: If your worship time is known for having a particular style, change it up the next time you lead. If it's technology-heavy, go tech-free. If it features lots of movement, have everyone be still. It doesn't need to be a permanent change, but breaking such routines sends the message that our enjoyment comes from *who* we worship, not *how* we worship. In fact, tell the kids that's why you're changing things.

Greeters, helpers, and mentors: The next time you're preparing to help at a ministry event, think of one kid and decide beforehand to encourage him or her with a brief comment about Jesus or the good news. Do this time after time, picking a different kid each time. Soon you'll be a great encourager.

Parents: You can be an encourager too. Each time you drop your kids off for a ministry event, tell them something about Jesus, or pray with them for their time in class. A quick, one-sentence prayer or encouragement is fine—it still sends a powerful message. And you too might keep the discussion questions from this chapter handy. They make good topics for the drive home as you ask your kids what they learned in class.

Chapter 9
The War on Sin and Bad Songs
Taking the good news into all of life

The oil of joy is poured chiefly into a broken heart.
—Thomas Watson[1]

I was fiddling around on my computer, checking for news from friends, when I noticed a highlighted bar indicating a personal message. Mail for me? I clicked to see who had written. It was a teenager I knew, Alex.

I was happy to hear from him. It'd been a few years since I'd taught Alex, but he'd been a good student. He liked the good news and was one of those kids who kept talking to me. We'd chat now and then at church. He seemed comfortable sharing with me, and I tried to be encouraging. Once my student, always my student, right?

For privacy's sake, I won't reprint his exact message. But he wrote something like this:

Hi, Mr. Klumpenhower,

What do you think of parties that have bad songs? Last night I was having fun, but now I see myself as a sinner. No one was drinking at the party, but some of my friends were singing and dancing to songs about sex and drugs, and I did too, and I was having fun. Now I feel guilty about it. Did I sin against God, or am I too hard on myself?

Alex went on to name a particular pop song he'd been dancing to and to tell me again how much fun he'd had and how much he felt like a sinner afterward. I didn't know the song, but I looked up the lyrics. Indeed, they were less than wholesome.

What should I tell him?

RELATIONSHIP-BASED . . . AND MORE

Before we look at how I responded to Alex, let me point out that none of us is a teacher for just an hour a week or only during organized family devotions. Those may be our planned sessions, but we teach full time. All we do, and every interaction with kids, teaches something.

Parents know this better than anyone. Our teaching comes alive as we share life with our kids and apply what we've learned. It's why spending time with our kids is just as important as teaching them the Bible. Workers in churches, clubs, camps, and other Christian organizations can share life with kids and their families as well. Many churches call this relationship-based ministry. That works for me—so long as we realize Jesus used an even stronger word.

One of the last, vital instructions Jesus gave his disciples was this: "A new commandment I give to you, that you love one another: just as I have loved you, you also are to love one another. By this all people will know that you are my disciples, if you have love for one another" (John 13:34–35). Jesus calls his people to *love*-based life together. The friendship and hospitality we associate with relationship-based ministry is the bare minimum. If Jesus has given us life with him, we must share our lives with others.

A Christian community is a collection of people who ordinarily wouldn't fit together but who nevertheless form deep fellowship in Christ. They share meals and homes and possessions. They confess sin and share burdens. In many churches this doesn't happen easily because people are isolated. Often the way they connect is through children's and youth ministry. Because of this teachers are uniquely positioned to welcome people into church fellowship. Your church needs you to do that.

Besides, it lets you speak into a kid's life. I'm shy so it's hard for me. But with my wife's help I've done things like invite families into my home and build true, lasting friendships. The kids from those families tend to be the ones who keep in touch. One result is that I get to help kids with faith and repentance outside the classroom—where they apply the lessons I'm teaching *in* the classroom.

Alex was one of those kids. His parents knew me and encouraged me to be part of his life. And he trusted me enough, apparently, to talk with me about his sin.

Who's the Enemy Here?

There were things I had to be careful *not* to say to Alex. First, it wouldn't do just to tell him what he was allowed to get away with. That's the wrong attitude for a follower of Jesus. Nor could I merely tell him what sin he needed to give up. Moral reform is not the same as Christian growth. Alex wanted a verdict on right and wrong behavior, but my answer had to go deeper than giving him rules.

Second, any idea that he was being too hard on himself and didn't need to deal with sin was the wrong way to think. Yes, a kid like Alex who's trying to measure up to God's standards seems miles ahead of one who doesn't care when he sins. But performing for God and ignoring God are both ways of bypassing Jesus. I couldn't tell Alex, "Well, since you wish you'd been better at sucking up to God, you're fine." Nor could I congratulate him for behaving better than the average kid. Sure, some kids attend far worse parties. But Alex probably *had* sinned, at least a little. Even if it was mild compared to other sin—and there's no guarantee it was—that's no reason to be satisfied. It was good that his conscience was bothered, and I had to urge him to listen to it.

Remember, the good news includes our transformation. We join the Holy Spirit's fight against sin in our lives—and we fight hard! Christians are at peace with God, yes. But this means we're also at war with sin. Our battle against sin is called repentance, and it's part of God's grace too. Believers still sin, sometimes severely, but what a blessing it is to bear Jesus's name and to have a new direction to life, choosing more and more to act like him!

Alex wasn't being too strict with himself. Fighting sin was the right idea. His problem was that his war with sin felt to him like war with God. He knew he should be less lewd at parties, but instead of feeling remorse, he felt condemned by God. He wished he could do better and prove himself worthy, but the sin was too much fun. He was frustrated, trying to impress God while secretly hoping for a free pass—yet sensing that his insecurity was somehow wrong too.

Alex needed to fight sin but to do it *with* God, instead of performing *for* God. He needed to hate sin but not keep a scorecard. He needed the good news.

WHAT I TOLD ALEX

The Bible uses many means of stirring up godly behavior. There are comforts and promises. There are also warnings, commands, and examples. A wise teacher knows his students and senses which of these to mention. He also knows when kids need to own up to the hard consequences that stem from sin.

I won't offer a complete guide to counseling kids in the many different struggles they face; I'm not qualified. I'm just here to remind you that whatever else you might say when talking with kids about their sin, don't leave out the good news. Never assume a kid already has it as his foundation. Pound it home.

The war on sin is not fought alone. Kids enlist in the battle alongside their Captain. This requires them to know and trust that he's on their side, not against them. Paul summarized his message as one "of repentance toward God and of faith in our Lord Jesus Christ" (Acts 20:21). Living for God means that repentance is knit together with faith.

With this in mind, what did I tell Alex? It went something like this:

Alex:

Hey, it's great to hear from you. I was excited to get your message.

I'm so glad you want to honor God in how you live, including the music you listen to and how you behave with your friends. We need to examine every part of our lives and always act according to our belief in Jesus. I'm glad you asked me about this, and I hope you're talking to your mom and dad about it too. They can help you figure out what honors God.

There probably was some sin in how you acted. Anytime we smell sin, it's usually there. So you might want to think about why your behavior felt so fun. What kind of selfishness was at the bottom of it? What did it seem to give you that you should be getting from Jesus? Find that, and repent of it. God gives the power you need to be able to resist that sin.

But as you do that, remember that you can't make God like you more by behaving better next time. And you can't make him more annoyed with you if you sin worse either. You need to give up all hope that your self-effort can make you perform to God's standards. Trust Jesus instead.

Never think that how God feels about you depends on how much dancing you did at a party or what the songs were—or any other behavior. How God feels about you depends on Jesus. Joined to Jesus, you're God's dearly loved child.

This means you and God are always on the same side. Even when you sin, he won't turn against you. So if your sin has hurt your relationship with your Father, go back to him. Tell him you're sorry. Be glad he forgives you! Pray and worship and feel his comfort.

Being close to your Father brings true sorrow for sin and helps you fight sin better next time. But even if you don't do better next time (and becoming more holy never seems to happen fast enough!), keep going back to him. Keep trusting Jesus. That's the main thing God's children do all the time—and the *best* thing we do.

God has the power and determination to kill off your sin. And he loves you in spite of your sin. So don't think you have to fight sin first so you can come to God. Instead, come to God so you can fight sin.

I'll pray for you. You may pray for me too because like you I sin sometimes by doing things I shouldn't just because they're fun. Together, I'm confident we'll learn to trust Jesus more and love him more. That makes it easier to hate sin. God *will* work this in us.

Let's get together and talk and pray sometime. I'd like that.

How did I do?

Before you decide, you need to know that I dropped the ball with Alex. My note suggested we meet to talk and pray, but I failed to follow through. Oh, I saw him at church and we chatted politely, but I got nervous and never set up anything more with him. I'd written a careful reply that had some good stuff in it, but then I gave in to my shyness and fear. I imagined a real talk and serious prayer might feel weird, and I got too scared to bring it up again. So I botched a good opportunity.

You should learn from my (bad) example. Be brave and trust God. Parents, pursue your kids. Teachers, pursue kids and their families when you have appropriate opportunities. Don't be a wimp like me.

Still, some good came out of my note to Alex. He thanked me for it and seemed to appreciate it. And in the years since then I've looked back at it when I've needed to remind myself what to say to other kids who struggle with sin. It contains four good-news principles for fighting sin that I try to keep in mind. Let's look at them now.

Four Principles for Fighting Sin

Principle #1: Focus on who you are in Jesus

When most people think of changing their behavior, they start with what they're already doing and then consider what needs to improve. Christians ought to think differently. Jesus is our beginning point. We build on him, not on our own starting behavior.

If we want believing kids to change how they act, we must teach them—perhaps counterintuitively—to focus *less* on how they act. We must first remind them *who they are*. They're joined to Jesus.

I sometimes test a kid by asking, "Imagine how God thinks of you today. What's the look on his face?"[2]

Almost always, kids see this as a question about how well they're measuring up to God's demands at the moment. Most won't dare claim they rate more than "pretty good" in God's eyes. Many tell me he's disappointed with them. This shows they have a performance mindset toward God. They're hoping they can be good enough, and God's holiness lax enough, to somehow measure up. It's pure foolishness.

I tell them they have no hope of making themselves good enough, but if they belong to Jesus, God always has a big smile when he thinks of them. They're counted righteous, forgiven through and through. They're God's children—cared for, provided for, died for.

I make much of the closeness we have to Jesus. They're not blessed from afar, as if he remained distant. No, they're wedded to him like a bride to her husband. Where he has rights and privileges and access, so do they. "[They] are fellow citizens with the saints and members of the household of God" (Ephesians 2:19).

The devil loves to challenge such statements. He'll point to kids' sin and try to tell them God's promise can't be true in their case. But the devil is a liar.

A kid's conscience may tell him he breaks every commandment. His heart may feel a constant tug toward evil. But the Word of God says that grasping Jesus by faith is never out of order and always works. Faith in Jesus trumps even repeated wrongdoing.

It's hard to believe God would give such repeated forgiveness or put up with us when we have to repent of the same thing again and again. Nor does anyone like to admit they keep failing. So kids tend to give up. They stop confessing and fighting certain sins. But far from being shameful, repeated repentance is a holy act that honors Jesus and the cross. His blood is powerful enough to cover repeat offenses.[3] "In Christ Jesus you who once were far off have been brought near by the blood of Christ" (Ephesians 2:13).

Alex needed to learn confidence in Christ's blood. His Christian life felt like a constant struggle to keep God from getting angry. He saw himself as a sinner trying to be holier. "Sinner" was his identity; "holy" was what he hoped to be someday.

But the Bible calls us "holy brothers, you who share in a heavenly calling" (Hebrews 3:1). "Holy" is who we are today in Jesus; "sinner" is a part of us that's a deviation from our true selves. Sin is something to repent of, but not what defines us. Paul tells us, "Consider yourselves dead to sin and alive to God in Christ Jesus" (Romans 6:11). Because sin doesn't always feel dead, I tell kids to keep considering what's true. "You're holy. Act the part. Praise God that he's already given you life to obey him in many ways. Trust that he'll make you grow even more."

The four categories of how the good news affects daily behavior (in our previous chapter) again come into play here:

- *Gratitude:* Is the kid's heart cold toward God? Teach him how his Father loves him in Jesus. Help him be *eager* to obey.
- *Confidence:* Is she frustrated with her progress? Tell her how the Spirit gives her power. Help her be *bold* about attacking even the toughest sin.
- *Hope:* Does he doubt that giving up sin is worth it? Urge him to believe God's promises in Christ. Help him be *enthusiastic* about serving God.
- *Comfort:* Is she worried God is mad at her? Assure her that her righteousness comes from Jesus. Help her be *unafraid* of God's commands.

Principle #2: Get beneath the surface

Once kids have the confidence that God isn't out to get them, they can dare to be brutally honest about their sin. Insecure kids aren't ready. They'll get defensive if you try to address deep sin. They'll insist you stay on the surface, where it's comfortable and easy to make excuses. Only a kid who's sure he's safe in Jesus will let you talk about the part of him that loves his sin, the ugliness inside.

At Serge, we often say sin is like a shark.[4] When a shark is swimming, the only part you see is the fin that sticks up above the water. But if you're hunting for that shark and want to kill it, you won't do much damage aiming at the fin. You need to aim below the fin where the shark's body is—under the surface.

It's the same with sin. The sin you can see—lies, angry outbursts, acts of greed, and such—are only surface stuff. The true monster responsible for them is lurking lower. We must never be content merely to help kids make their surface sins less obvious or frequent.

The shark illustration works so well that I've started sketching shark pictures for kids and walking them through the process of looking under the surface. I begin with the obvious sin they can see. If I'd gotten around to this with Alex, the surface sin in his case would be enjoying lewd music with his friends. I'd write this sin next to the shark's fin in my sketch.

Surface sin I can see:
Enjoying bad songs with friends

Next we look beneath the surface. Alex needed to see that his sin wasn't just that he broke a rule—"Don't act lewdly." He needed to see that something in his heart was opposed to God and produced that sin. It might have been idolatry—a selfish desire for something that made him feel good and came before Jesus in his life. Alex never told me what idol led to his lewd singing, but let's suppose it was the charge he got from the suggestiveness of the songs. He loved that energy more than he loved Jesus.

Whatever the selfish desire is, I write it next to the shark under the surface.

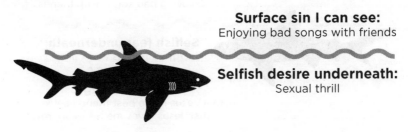

Surface sin I can see:
Enjoying bad songs with friends

Selfish desire underneath:
Sexual thrill

If a kid can't pinpoint a selfish *desire*, sometimes it's easier to identify a selfish *fear*. He might be scared he'll lose something that makes him feel secure or important. In Alex's case, maybe he wasn't falling for sexual temptation at all. Instead, he might have been afraid his friends wouldn't like him if he didn't behave the way they did.

If that's the case, that's what I write next to the shark.

Surface sin I can see:
Enjoying bad songs with friends

Selfish fear underneath:
Afraid friends won't like
or accept me

Now comes the deepest level. Both selfish desires and selfish fears arise because we fail to fully believe the good news of what Jesus gives us. Why was Alex looking to suggestive lyrics to get a thrill? Because he didn't fully believe that intimacy with Jesus is even more exciting. Nor did he deeply believe that the pure in heart will see God.

Or, why was he afraid that his friends might disapprove of him? Because he didn't fully believe that he already has the world's best possible friend in Jesus, and God's perfect approval. If he did believe this, he wouldn't feel a need to seek approval from lewd friends.

Let's use this example to finish the illustration. *Failure to believe in Jesus* is the deepest level of sin. It goes at the bottom.

Surface sin I can see:
Enjoying bad songs with friends

Selfish fear underneath:
Afraid friends won't like
or accept me

Not believing...
...that Jesus is the best friend I could have
...that Jesus gives me *God's* approval

This works with any surface sin.

- *Does the kid tease other kids?* Maybe she's made an idol out of being part of the preferred crowd. She needs to believe that her inclusion in God's family is the best honor she could hope for.
- *Does he always grab the biggest slice of pizza?* Maybe he's greedy for the things of this world. He needs to believe that treasures stored up in heaven are surely his in Christ.
- *Does she gossip about other girls? Does she dress suggestively?* Maybe she's insecure and envies the attention others get. She needs to believe that Jesus's Father is her Father too, who loves her perfectly.
- *Does he get angry when he loses a game?* Maybe he worships being first in worldly things. He needs to believe that he's been raised with Christ and seated with him in the heavenly places.
- *Does she lie to her parents?* Maybe she can't handle being corrected. She needs to believe that she's counted righteous in Jesus no matter how badly she messes up at home. Or maybe she's hiding other sin. She needs to believe that the discipline God puts in her life is loving and good for her.

I try to be gentle when pointing out unbelief, so kids won't just feel scolded. Still, it's important that they deal with more than surface sins.

They might manage to suppress those sins for a while, but the behavior will surely come back—because the shark is still there.

Principle #3: Rely on the Spirit

Belief is critical in battling sin because no matter how hard a kid tries, he'll get no further than as far as he trusts. It's the Holy Spirit who changes kids. He brings rebirth at the start of the Christian life and then more and more holiness as that life goes on. Jesus said, "Apart from me you can do nothing" (John 15:5). Paul wrote, "It is no longer I who live, but Christ who lives in me" (Galatians 2:20). Alex needed to see that he had no power in himself to conquer sin, but unlimited power as a child of God.

Sure, maybe Alex could have hunkered down and, in his own power, started avoiding certain parties. Plenty of kids do that sort of thing—and to an extent, for a while, it might work. Even unbelievers can make themselves more moral. But they can't make themselves *holier*. No one can.

I wanted Alex confidently battling sin in *God's* strength—because God would change his core person. Self-reliance is the enemy of that kind of growth. Willpower stands in its way. It wasn't enough for Alex to try to increase his ability to obey God. He needed to aim *beyond* his ability. He needed to trust the Spirit, who had both the power and the loving desire to make him holy inside and out. Such trust is never, ever misplaced. Paul teaches, "Walk by the Spirit, and you will not gratify the desires of the flesh" (Galatians 5:16).

So if a kid's main job is to trust the Spirit, what can you urge him to *do*? What does trust look like, and how can a kid work hard at it?

The answer is that he can seek God relentlessly. He can practice disciplines that connect him with the tools God typically uses in a believer's life to beat back sin and produce growth. These ordinary tools of the Spirit are (1) the Word of God and (2) prayer.

To connect kids with the Word of God, we must urge them to read their Bibles. I've heard people say that they don't care much for

Bible study, preferring to "follow the Spirit" instead. The Spirit *wrote* the Bible. When kids read the Bible, intending to submit their lives to it and embrace its good news, *that's following the Spirit*. That's making their own thoughts captive to the Spirit's Word so that they're free to live in him.

They can also hear the Word of God when a minister called by God preaches it. And they can see, feel, and taste it in the church's ordinances or sacraments—the Communion meal and baptism. We ought to encourage kids to attend church worship services. They should go in faith, trusting and expecting God to work.

The second tool—prayer—is the foundational behavior of a dependent believer. We must pray, pray, pray with kids. We must teach them to pray with others and on their own—to pray without ceasing. This idea is so crucial to good-news teaching that I devote the entire next chapter to it.

Because I pound home the value of prayer, Bible reading, and churchgoing, I also give kids two warnings about them. You need to keep these in mind as well.

The Spirit's tools aren't magic. Don't make the mistake of approaching them the way you'd prescribe a pill, as if merely repeating prayers or Bible verses gives a sprinkling of spiritual pixie dust. No, the tools work because by them kids engage the Spirit—who is a person. They must meet him with their hearts. He, not his tools, is the source of power.

The Spirit's tools aren't for bargaining with God. It's right to put a huge emphasis on these disciplines, but watch out. Kids might start to feel like they have to read the Bible a certain amount each day or pray for so long, or else God will be mad at them. Don't let these disciplines become burdensome duties—or worse, manipulative ones. Help kids see that they're a hope-filled sort of duty, bringing them close to God and tapping into his power. They're oxygen for running the race.

Principle #4: Seek God himself

A life immersed in God's Word and prayer brings closeness to God. That must be the ultimate issue. The only thing that can give any kid deep joy is the assurance that God knows him—including his struggles and ugly sins—and still loves him.

I wanted Alex to forcefully go after the very best God offers—God himself.

A wife appreciates getting roses and chocolates from her husband. She enjoys the legal and social benefits of her married status too. But what does she want most of all? She treasures sharing life with her husband. Marriage is about the person you're with.

It's the same with God. Alex needed to run to embrace him. Anything less just tempts kids to fake repentance. They'll work on looking good while secretly wishing they could still get away with sin. They'll mock God with "repentance" that's all talk and no change. Or they'll put on a performance to try to finagle from God the blessings they really want more than they want him—and never have true sorrow for their sin.

Drawing near to your Father by faith in the good news of Jesus—getting to know his blinding holiness and his unblinking love—is altogether different. *That* brings sharp awareness of sin. Sorrow for wrongdoing. A grieving soul. Tears. Confession. Acceptance of blame. An end to excuses. The sweet mercy of godly shame. A grip on Jesus. Joy in forgiveness. Grateful love for God and for all things godly. Hatred of sin and all things ungodly.

And it brings eagerness to obey. Turning from sin is the *last* step. That doesn't mean we put it off; God gives power *now*, and turning from sin is urgent. But full repentance flourishes only when hearts are broken and close to God. Then we grow in grace. Then repentance becomes joy.

QUESTIONS YOU MIGHT BE ASKING

You talk about fighting sin by believing in Jesus and trusting him. But shouldn't kids also try hard not to sin? Shouldn't there be a balance between trusting and doing?

No. It's the wrong approach to do a little trusting and a little active running from sin, as if those two acts were opposites. It doesn't work that way. They go together. We must tell kids to strive hard to conquer sin in their lives and serve God: "Press on toward the goal" (Philippians 3:14). But the power to do this comes from God, so they must also trust him and rest in his promises—steadily and obsessively. More trusting leads to more doing. There's no balance, as if too much trusting will hamper doing. The Christian life is both—all out and all the time.

It sounds strange for you to say that repentance is part of God's grace to us. Isn't grace what God does for us, while repentance is something we do?

Actually, the Bible lumps our God-given opportunity to repent in with other parts of the good news, like Jesus's death and resurrection and our forgiveness. "Thus it is written, that the Christ should suffer and on the third day rise from the dead, and that repentance and forgiveness of sins should be proclaimed in his name to all nations" (Luke 24:46–47). The call to repent is a beautiful gift from God and, as I've mentioned, the act of repentance is always done *with* him, relying on him.

In your conversation with Alex, you seemed to treat him as if you were sure he was a believer, telling him he was joined to Jesus and God's child. Are you sure he was a believer?

Well, he professed to be a believer, so I treated him like one. You can never be sure, but like I've said before, it often doesn't make that much difference in what you say to a kid. If he wasn't saved, telling him the good news and counseling him to believe it and repent was still the right thing. At some point you need to accept that a kid is a believer when he claims to be one, especially when he confesses faith in Jesus and shows some basic evidence of repentance by wanting to fight sin in his life. If you're always questioning his salvation, you end up questioning God's faithfulness to him—just like the devil does. That will hurt rather than help.

What about kids who show little or no concern for their sin? Do you take a different approach?

They have to see their sin and be convicted of it. The shark diagram and lots of time spent reading the Bible help, but all kids need to repent throughout their life. Some especially need to repent of a sinful lifestyle. Others especially need to repent of a self-justifying, prove-I'm-good-enough approach to God. With the church kids I usually teach, I find the need for the second kind of repentance is often the harder concept to grasp.

Show Them Jesus Right Away

Act now to apply the good news in all parts of your life with kids. Here are some suggestions:

Parents: With your older kids, use the shark diagram the next time you have to discuss a recurring behavior problem. If confessing sin and encouraging each other with the good news are not already common in your family, you might need to show that it's safe to openly discuss sin by first sharing an example of your *own* behavior problems. On the shark diagram, (1) write out one of your surface sins, (2) write out what idols or fears are underneath that sin, and (3) write out the unbelief in Jesus that is at the bottom of it all. Then take your child through the exercise. Resist telling what *you* think is going on in his or her heart. Instead, give your child time to think and express it. Once you've explored the sin "under the surface," it's usually good to end with prayer for God to work repentance or with some other encouragement to believe. The goal of the exercise is to bring repentance that goes beneath surface sins to include idols, fears, and unbelief.

Your ability to guide your child toward godly behavior at the heart level will increase with the amount of quality time you and the child spend together and the exposure your child gets to the Holy Spirit's ordinary tools that bring growth—God's Word and prayer. Examine your family schedule and activities. Map out your time together. Are you satisfied that it's enough time and good time, or do you feel busy and disconnected? Is there ample room for your family to frequently pray, read the Bible, and worship together? Do you and each child regularly join in these things with your church too? If you can't give answers you feel good about, take a hard look at what activities and commitments interfere—and pick some to get rid of! Cut back at least one commitment a week *now*. If the situation doesn't improve, cut back more. You may have to reduce both *your* activities and those of your kids. But it's worth it.

Youth leaders: The kids you lead can fill out the shark diagram, described for parents above. They should be able to appreciate your attempt to look beyond surface sins. Sometimes it works well to first use impersonal examples in a group setting: "What if someone sins a lot by bragging—what idols or fears might be under the surface? What is that person not believing about Jesus?" Then, when you have a chance later to talk to a kid more privately, you can use the shark to discuss that kid's particular sin.

For younger kids: Little kids will have a difficult time naming the idols and fears beneath their surface sins—but they understand them! So when correcting a young child's surface sins, ask about the deeper reality too. You'll probably have to suggest a likely motivation and use child-friendly language, for example:

- Instead of "envy" . . . "Did you want that just because someone else had it?"
- Instead of "greed" . . . "Did you want the most for yourself?"
- Instead of "self-pride" . . . "Did you want me to think you were better than you really are?"
- Instead of "lust" . . . "Did you think having that would make you happy?"

Once you identify the right motivation, assure him or her that you understand it. "All people feel that way sometimes, but we don't *have* to feel that way." Tell what Jesus has done for us that makes the motivation unnecessary. "You don't have to get the most for yourself because Jesus is planning to share everything he has with us." With repeated reminders, even young kids will learn to believe in Jesus as an essential part of their fight against sin.

Teachers: Teach kids about the importance of the Spirit's ordinary tools by preparing a toolbox, backpack, or school desk drawer and labeling it "Holy Spirit supplies." Ask kids to guess what supplies the Spirit gives that help them grow as believers. After some guesses, open the object to reveal a Bible (God's written Word), an item representing church services (God's Word preached, baptism, and Communion), and a picture or figurine of praying hands. Explain that the Spirit gives us these things to keep us connected to Jesus and growing. This is a good way to show that prayers, Bible reading, and churchgoing aren't chores we do to impress God, but gifts we use to grow in Christ.

Chapter 10
The Class in the Boiler Room
Living the good news through prayer

The great duty of prayer is to catch a sight of God in heaven,
and Christ at his right hand.
—Thomas Manton[1]

Several years ago my church met in a large, old building in the middle of the city. It was a good location for ministry, but sometimes we had trouble with trespassers and vandals. They'd break into the building at night and commit small acts of mischief.

One time the vandals got into the children's area, made a little shrine, and set fire to a giant teddy bear we had in there. That was spooky. Now the problem was serious. We couldn't hide it from the kids, who were nervous about it. Some of the littlest ones cried over the bear.

A few weeks later a fellow teacher came up to me before Sunday school. She had an idea. She was planning to take her class to the building's boiler room, which had an outdoor entrance and was a repeated target of the vandals, and there they would pray. It'd be a long prayer meeting, taking most of class time. They'd pray for the vandals. They'd pray for the building to be secure. They'd pray for God to comfort their fears. They might even pray for the boiler itself, which had a habit of conking out and leaving us in the cold.

"Would your class like to come too?" she asked.

I hesitated. I didn't want to.

"You can think about it and let me know," she said.

But I didn't have to think about it. I already knew I didn't want my class to pray in the boiler room. I just didn't know how to tell her without looking unspiritual.

WHY WE DON'T LIKE TO PRAY

There might have been some good reasons for not wanting to join that prayer time, but *my* reasons were bad ones. For starters, I was too proud to jump at something that wasn't my idea. Beyond that, the whole thing sounded like it might get uncomfortable.

I did pray regularly with my class, of course, but I preferred short, routine, safe prayers. My students might think the prayer in the boiler room was over the top or silly. Or they might get bored. And surely I, as the teacher, would be on the spot to participate and say some impressive-sounding prayers—which I didn't do as well as teaching Bible lessons.

The prayer sounded risky too. Suppose the vandalism got worse. What would I tell the kids? Wouldn't it look like the prayer didn't work, or like we hadn't prayed well enough? Serious prayer messed with my gotta-look-good, performance mindset toward teaching. Plus, it got tedious. It tended to drag on longer than I had the energy for.

Let me come out and say it: I just didn't *like* prayer.

I knew I *should* like it. After all, prayer was part of Jesus's own ministry to kids. "Children were brought to him that he might lay his hands on them and pray" (Matthew 19:13). People forget that line, but I hadn't. I also knew that prayer is "the chief exercise of faith."[2] We're saved by trusting God instead of ourselves, and we must also live the Christian life by trusting God instead of ourselves. That's faith—and prayer shows you have it.

I knew all this, and yet I decided to wiggle out of taking my class to pray. I made some excuse and just taught my prepared lesson, whatever it was.

Of course, it was no surprise when the other teacher saw me later and told me what a fine experience the prayer time had been for her class. They had taken their concerns to God and practiced trusting him. She was an excellent teacher. She loved to pray, and it rubbed off on her students.

I didn't. I preferred things to be about myself. And although I wouldn't have admitted it, I found talking to God boring. I didn't just avoid prayer with my class—I seldom prayed alone either. My grasp of God's majesty was sorely lacking. So was my sense of my sin, the cost Jesus incurred to bear it, and my utter weakness apart from him. I wasn't living out the good news.

FEELING GUILTY ABOUT PRAYER

I've grown since then, but I'm still not very good at prayer. Yet here I am, writing about it. Partly, that's because no book on teaching about Jesus could possibly be complete without a section on prayer. Most importantly, though, it's because I know there are many, many other teachers like me. If you struggle to want to pray, you're not alone. I won't scold you.

We shouldn't be surprised that prayer is a struggle. Since it's the core of the life of faith, we can expect the devil to attack our prayer lives. If he can get us to avoid prayer, we'll be flimsy teachers. We'll be hypocrites—telling kids to trust God while we actually trust ourselves and telling them how wonderful God is while we treat him as unworthy of our time.

Since being a prayerless teacher *is* that bad, it's easy to feel guilty about how poorly we pray. This means you and I need to remember—always, always when we pray—that God has set up prayer to do the opposite, to *never* make us feel guilty. Convicted? Yes. But guilty? No. Our prayer should never condemn us, no matter how bad we are at it. Want proof? It's plain in what the Bible says about prayer.

WHY PRAYER SHOULD NEVER FEEL CONDEMNING

Prayer gives us access only through Jesus.

God doesn't hear our prayers because we prayed well. We're only able to pray in the first place because we're joined to Jesus. Jesus sits at the Father's right hand, vouching for us! *He* is good. His blood makes us welcome: "Let us then with confidence draw near to the throne of grace, that we may receive mercy and find grace to help in time of need" (Hebrews 4:16). Yes, our coldness toward God is horrible, but we may still pray. Doing so is proof of how fully we're forgiven—even for not praying. Do you see? God designed prayer to remind us how righteous we are in Christ, not what failures we are.

Prayer involves the Spirit's help.

God doesn't hang around to scold us for shabby or too-short prayers. He knows we're weak, so he's our partner in prayer: "The Spirit helps us in our weakness. For we do not know what to pray for as we ought, but the Spirit himself intercedes for us with groanings too deep for words" (Romans 8:26). We don't need to try to be impressive; we can be honest with our partner. We can admit to God how hard prayer is. He won't condemn us. He *expects* us to need assistance.

Prayer is a Father-and-child experience.

When the disciples asked Jesus to teach them to pray, he began by teaching them to call God "Father." Being joined to Jesus means sharing the same Father. God is eager to hear our prayers, no matter how childish our prayer life is. We enter into the loving Father-child fellowship that Jesus has always known. Condemnation falls away and is replaced by delight.

This means that if you feel dishonest, hypocritical, callous, standoffish, stubborn, proud, lazy, unworthy, uncaring, or any of the other condemning things I feel when I think about *my* prayer life—well then, you need to pray. Prayer is for exactly that kind of mule-headed jerk. Prayer is where all that dissolves and sinners rest in grace.

No Threats, No Need to Impress

As a guy who's still learning to pray, I urge you to forget about your poor track record. Don't let your cold heart stop you. Let Jesus be all that qualifies you to pray.

Throughout eternity, Jesus has enjoyed depending on the Father and sharing every thought with him. Now *you* are joined to Jesus. You have the same privilege of coming to your Father anytime to tell him anything—in any condition. Believe it, and pray! Never imagine that God holds prayer over your head, threatening to make your life go badly or make your ministry fail if you don't pray often enough and sincerely enough. That kind of prayer just makes life harder. It isn't how Jesus prays, and you pray *in him*.

Elijah is one of our examples in prayer. "He prayed fervently that it might not rain, and for three years and six months it did not rain on the earth" (James 5:17). He prayed for God to bring a boy back to life. He prayed on Mount Carmel that the Lord would send fire from heaven. He prayed when he was struggling too—on the run from Queen Jezebel, he once prayed that he might die. Instead, God came and gave him strength and encouragement.

Elijah's life and ministry were powerful because he depended on God in prayer. But my favorite thing about Elijah is the difference between his prayer to the true God and the false prayers of the priests of Baal. On Mount Carmel, the priests of Baal begged all day for their god to send fire first. "They cried aloud and cut themselves after their custom with swords and lances, until the blood gushed out upon them" (1 Kings 18:28). They were acting as their god required. A Baal-worshiper's prayer meant doing something for Baal so he'd answer. Cry loudly. Maim yourself. Do *something, anything*, to get him to listen.

May we never take that approach with the true God! Our God does not require us to bleed for him; he bled for us. He's so much better than a Baal—not fake but real, not weak but powerful, not harsh but compassionate. Best of all, he's different from every false god the world has imagined because he doesn't ask, "What have you done for me?" He declares "Here's what *I've* done for *you*."

It's our duty to pray to God. Certainly. He's due it. No doubt. But the main reason he's put it in place is because he's our Father. He loves to see the profits of prayer flow back to us.[3]

THE PRAYERFUL TEACHER

You and I have every reason, then, to be prayerful teachers. It must start with private prayer. We must learn to spend time alone with our Father. We must come to enjoy it. As the boiler-room incident taught me, you can't have prayer-centered teaching without a prayer-happy teacher.

Prayerful teachers I've talked to learned to pray in many different ways. I don't know what'll work for you, except that you have to start by believing the good news. Prayer is weakness tapping into power, so use prayer to trust Jesus instead of yourself. Pray for the Spirit to inject new power into both your life and your teaching, and believe that he's eager to do it.

If you're a particularly bookish teacher, like me, who likes studying the Bible but has a hard time diving into prayer, try reading the Psalms. Those are the best prayers. I'll sometimes pick a psalm or some other prayer in the Bible and start studying it, letting it move me into praying those words back to God. The Psalms are one way the Spirit helps us. He's given us a prayer book for times when we don't know how to pray.

Beyond that, I won't pretend to give you a formula for successful private prayer. That'd be like telling you how to talk with your spouse. You need to follow your heart, not a manual. I do have some ideas, though, for introducing your life of prayer to kids and teaching them to pray.

Idea #1: On-the-Spot Prayer

If you do only one thing to add fuel to your prayer ministry, I suggest on-the-spot prayer. By this I mean that when a kid or group tells you about a problem or voices some concern, stop and pray about it with them right then and there. If it happens during teaching time, stop teaching and pray. If it happens outside of class or group, stop and pray. At home or away, at church or around town, if a kid mentions a need, pray with that kid.

This teaches kids that our hope is in God—for little things, for big things, for *everything*. It says every part of ministry and life is always in concert with God, and it builds a habit of turning first to him—faith as a knee-jerk reaction. This kind of prayer enjoys and uses the access to the Father that Jesus has won for us. Nothing is more basic to living out the good news.

If that kind of prayer culture hasn't taken root where you teach or in your home, on-the-spot prayer will feel awkward at first. That worry has stopped me from praying on countless occasions. I urge you to do better. Pray with kids anyway. You're their teacher, or their parent. You should be praying. Do it and you'll get used to it—and so will those around you.

In many situations, prayer is the only viable option. Recently I was teaching large-group lessons at a vacation Bible school. As the kids gathered for singing time, I noticed a girl I knew sitting alone on one side of the room, quietly crying. I crouched down next to her and asked what was wrong. She was a bit too eager to tell me. Her sister had been mean to her at home. Her mom had done nothing about it. And now she was afraid her friends didn't like her.

Like I say, I knew this girl. She had a tendency to whine. I didn't want to blindly affirm her or agree that her sister and mom had done wrong. Still, maybe they had. There was no way for me to know, and it wasn't my business anyway. The girl was upset, and my job was to help her without taking sides.

I relied on habit. I asked if I could pray for her. She said yes, and we prayed right there. I asked God to help her and her family be kind to each other. I prayed they would be able to forgive each other. I prayed the same for her and her friends. That was all. It was short but serious. When I was done I could tell she felt better already. She actually thanked me.

Please don't think I prayed with her because I wanted to brush aside her issues and be done with her. No, I prayed because that was what she needed in that situation. We had to turn to the Father, who knows all hearts. It was a moment for God to handle, rather than me. The best thing I could teach her in that setting was that God listens when we're sad and angry, and he helps.

Opportunities like that come up all the time. That time I remembered to pray. If you look for opportunities, you will remember too.

Idea #2: No-Rules Prayer

When I lead group prayer in class, we often operate under what I call "no-rules" prayer. This means that basic behavior rules still apply, but there are no special rules for prayer time. You don't have to close eyes, fold hands, or bow heads. Also, you can pray about whatever you like, as long as it isn't clearly sinful. The point is to make sure no kid thinks prayer is about impressing God with a pious posture, fancy words, or noble concerns. I want to build a habit of coming to the Father with any need at all or any bit of thanks, unfiltered, whether or not it makes a kid look mature and spiritual.

Especially with younger kids, this means I often have to bite my tongue. I'm tempted to rate their prayers. I think prayer for Alicia's grandma who has cancer is better than the prayer Brian just requested for his scratched knee. I judge Joel's prayer for missionaries more important than Heather's prayer that her cat will learn to stop jumping on the furniture.

There *is* a sense in which some prayers are weightier than others. But the no-rules method affirms that any prayer that takes hopes and anxieties and turns them over to the Father is an excellent one. If a kid cares for his dog, he should pray for his dog. As he matures, his concerns will turn to weightier things—though I hope his prayers will still be freewheeling and unguarded. I want him constantly turning to his Father with life's cares, both big and small, both mature and childlike—"casting all your anxieties on him, because he cares for you" (1 Peter 5:7).

Sometimes I've tried to enlarge kids' vision for prayer by giving a list of the sorts of things they can ask from God. Categories include the following:

- help when there's trouble
- daily care
- help to become more godly
- salvation for people who aren't Christians
- the church's work and mission
- leaders and people in charge

Without the list, I've found that kids seldom think past the first two categories. I like to broaden their view by telling them that the Bible mentions prayer for all these things, plus prayers of thanks and praise and confession. That said, I always put the list away if I catch kids trying to cover every topic, as if that makes their prayers better. It never does. It just turns prayer into a performance.

Tip #3: *Your* Ideas for Prayer

There are plenty more time-tested ways to pray with kids. I've prayed as they've arrived. I've prayed as they've left. I've prayed as we've transitioned between activities. I've invited other groups to pray with us. I've invited other adults in to pray for us. I've invited missionaries to visit class so we could pray for them. I also know several teachers who have their students keep a prayer journal. All good ideas.

I could give you more—but it's even better, I think, if you come up with your own ideas. The real struggle is not figuring out when and where and how to pray. It's *wanting* to pray. If you want to pray, you'll think of all kinds of good ways to do it.

James tells us, "You do not have, because you do not ask" (James 4:2). The obvious follow-up is why don't I ask more often? It's because I'm still proud and prefer to rely on myself. I don't like to depend on anyone. Not even God.

I'm still learning the hard way. Perhaps you are too. So I say, learn to be shameless like the man in Jesus's story who pounded on his friend's door at midnight asking for bread. Even that selfish friend got out of bed and helped—and you have a better Friend who's selfless and giving. Jesus *lives* to intercede for you; he will surely hurry to answer you.

And you will gain much more than all you ask. You will meet with God himself. That's the goal of salvation in Jesus. God wants us to be with him. When we get to prayer, we've reached our destination.

SHOW THEM JESUS RIGHT AWAY

Before anything else, if you're at all like me and find prayer difficult, I'd like you to stop reading for just a moment and pray. Tell your Father how you feel about prayer and ask him to help you pray better. Go ahead. Do it right now.

—pause for prayer—

Now that you've started talking with your Father, consider what else you'll do to make more of prayer in your work with kids. One of the ideas below might make a good start.

Parents: There's no place on-the-spot prayer makes a bigger difference than in the home. Start implementing it today. Whenever someone's worried or voices a concern—no matter how small—take a moment to pray about it. Often it'll be a very quick prayer you say while you keep working or driving (though it doesn't *have* to be short). If you're concerned that you'll be pausing to pray several times day—you're right! It's a good way to "pray without ceasing" (1 Thessalonians 5:17), and it will create in your family a sense of constant dependence on God and an appreciation of living with him.

Teachers and group leaders: If the kids you work with seem un-comfortable with prayer, or self-conscious about praying aloud, re-lieve the pressure by eliminating some of the rules (stated or assumed) that govern prayer time. Don't force kids to use a certain posture or tone of voice, and be especially careful not to judge prayers—either by what was said or how spiritual it sounded. The moment you tell a kid, "That was beautiful," you turn prayer into a performance and heighten the tension for everyone. Instead, work to shift the appreciation of prayer away from who said what and how it was said, and toward joy in being able to bring *any* praise or concern before our Father.

Ministry leaders: Do some prayer-idea sharing the next time your ministry team gets together. Ask fellow teachers, group leaders, coun-selors, and mentors to share prayer-time ideas that have worked for them with kids. You might also brainstorm ways to get kids involved in meaningful prayer. Ask one another *who* might we invite to pray with us, or who might come in and let us pray for them? *Where* might we pray? *How* might we keep track of our prayers? Just fifteen minutes of sharing could produce a wealth of creative ideas.

Anyone: If the kids you pray with seem bored with the same old kinds of prayer requests, consider enlarging their vision for prayer by suggesting categories of things the Bible says we can pray for. Here's the list again:

- help when there's trouble
- daily care
- help to become more godly
- salvation for people who aren't Christians
- the church's work and mission
- leaders and people in charge

You could ask them, "What godly behavior do you want to do better that we can pray for?" or, "What work that the church is doing shall we pray about?" and see what suggestions they come up with. Just be careful not to let it become a contest to come up with the best ideas. Whatever concern is already on a kid's heart always makes the best prayer request.

One way to become more prayerful is to add quick occasions for prayer to your daily routine. Many people pray every time they eat. You might also consider (1) greeting your Father as soon as you wake up in the morning, (2) praying for your day when you get in the car or sit down to start work, (3) sharing concerns or thanks at bedtime, or (4) praying any other time that fits your schedule. The point is to get in the habit of praying *often* throughout the day. Do that and you'll develop a more constant sense of your Father's presence. It will make you more likely to respond prayerfully to any situation that pops up at any point in the day.

Chapter 11

The Skis I Never Wore

Making the good news your great hope

Fear not; only, believe, wait, and pray. Expect not all at once. A Christian is not of hasty growth, like a mushroom, but rather like the oak, the progress of which is hardly perceptible, but, in time, becomes a great deep-rooted tree.

—John Newton[1]

I was sipping coffee and greeting friends before church when one of my students, a teenaged boy, walked up to me. It wasn't unusual for him to say hello. I liked him and he liked me. I asked him how things were going, but he hadn't come to chit-chat. He had an invitation for me.

He and his family were going skiing later that week. Would I like to come along and ski with them? He looked at me with raised eyes, clearly begging for a yes.

"Uh . . ." Well, what *would* I say?

THE PROBLEM WITH SKIING

Here's what you need to know. I can't ski.

I live in Colorado, where it seems like everyone skis—everyone but me. I've been on skis once in my life, years ago, and it was a painful experience—both hard on my body and hurtful to my pride. I was a slow learner, uncoordinated, and I decided then and there that I didn't like skiing. I've never been back.

When people ask me to ski, I usually tell them that I don't. If they push, I admit that I never learned and don't want to try. This kid, though, came from a family that was nuts about skiing. He'd probably started learning when he was three. In his mind, I guessed, someone who didn't know how to ski was like a guy who never learned to ride a bike—a total, wussy loser.

No way was I going skiing with that kid. Nor would I tell him I couldn't ski. He might be nice about it and offer to teach me, and that could only be more embarrassing.

"Um, I really don't like skiing very much," I told him. "And I'm sure I'm not very good at it compared to you."

"That's okay," he said. "We don't care. Please come."

"No, skiing just isn't my thing."

His eyes fell. I had told him, in effect, that I didn't want to spend time with him doing something he found fun. He never asked me again.

TEACH THE GOOD NEWS—TO YOURSELF

I bungled that invitation in so many ways. Let's start with how I failed to take advantage of an obvious opportunity to build my relationship with that boy and his parents. My first consideration was avoiding embarrassment. It was my idol. I put it ahead of serving God. Even more deeply, my insecurity showed that I failed to believe the good news. The reputation Jesus gives me with God wasn't enough for me, so I lied to protect my worldly reputation.

I didn't *do* what I teach. I didn't rest in the righteousness of Jesus. I failed to see and love him, or humble myself in response to him. I was a fraud as a teacher, advertising living water without drinking it myself.

Let's not kid ourselves. Students sense the difference between a teacher with integrity and a fake. There's nothing they demand more than integrity. Not hipness. Not entertainment. Not even solid Bible teaching. They want—and need—for us to be practicing believers in everyday life. They want us to be like Paul, who said, "Our gospel came to you not only in word, but also in power and in the Holy Spirit and with full conviction. You know what kind of men we proved to be among you for your sake" (1 Thessalonians 1:5).

To teach the good news in that way is a daunting demand. I mess it up regularly. In spite of our sinful blunders, though, we should not despair. The good news gives us tremendous hope. We can repent—daily, hourly, constantly. We can treasure God's forgiveness over and over. We can believe that he counts us as saints and loves us as sons, and then we can believe bigger. We can be revived.

Sure, we catch ourselves serving idols and putting our fears ahead of God's promises. But growth as a Christian is not about getting to a point where we stop sinning so much and do better on our own. It's more about learning to depend on Jesus constantly, increasing in faith, and trusting him in our weakness. We need to teach the good news not just to our students but first to our own hearts. For me, this has to happen again and again. Every day.

A BAD WEEK AT CAMP

A few years ago I taught at a week-long Bible camp in the mountains. There were a few dozen preteen campers, a handful of teenaged helpers, some counselors, camp leaders, and me, the teacher.

I soon became frustrated. The kids weren't responding to my lessons the way I was used to. I knew who to blame too—the teen helpers. I was used to helpers who took an interest in a camp's Bible content so they could talk about it with the younger kids during free time, but these helpers acted like they didn't care. They didn't bother sitting in on my lessons. Some would even walk through our meeting area while I was trying to teach, and they became a distraction.

I'd been in charge of preparing a booklet to guide each camper through personal devotions each morning. My understanding had been that the teen helpers would use the booklet too, and I'd taken pains to include material that'd be meaningful for them. But most never joined in devotions; they slept late, did chores, or sat around talking while the younger kids had their quiet time. One morning a couple of them were even tossing water balloons.

The camp director reminded me that the helpers had chores that caused them to lose sleep or to be busy during lesson time, and that he was addressing behavior issues in a way he hoped was good for the helpers' hearts. He was right, of course. It wasn't all about me. So I tried not to complain. I didn't want to look like a selfish teacher who couldn't handle a few distractions.

Inside, though, I simmered. No one was marveling at my teaching. My reputation was suffering, and those helpers who should have been better examples—and who should have been appreciating *me*—well, they needed to shape up!

SIN SPILLS OUT

One afternoon the campers were playing water games. The helpers were supposed to be assisting, but they seemed more interested in continuing their own water balloon battle from the morning before. I saw one guy run right into the campers' game, chasing another helper with a bucket of water. I exploded.

I pulled him aside. "You're supposed to be helping," I snapped at him. "You've been selfish and thinking about your own fun when your job is to be here for the younger kids. Stop putting yourself first!" He was a bit stunned, but he got the message. He hadn't actually been one of the worst offenders that week, but it was about time one of those helpers got set straight.

I knew I was sinning, of course. Somewhere in the back of my mind I even knew that I was chiefly the one being selfish, lashing out because my dreams of glory through my teaching had been upset. At the moment I didn't care. It felt too satisfying to stop.

It wasn't until the next morning that I was ready to confront *my* sin. Camp was winding down. I was preparing a lesson and campfire talk that would urge kids to abandon their pride and embrace the good news they'd heard that week, and to go home with renewed love for Jesus and zeal to serve him.

God is funny that way sometimes.

He gave me grace that morning. Countless times I've taught kids without first coming to grips with the good news in my own heart. This time, I saw my sinful self and took it to my Savior. I was critical, and I admitted it. I considered myself better than others in camp and thought myself the best guy to judge their behavior. I was prideful so that when my lessons didn't work well enough to feed that pride, I became annoyed. I worshiped the idea of being a good teacher. I craved classes that were orderly and students who learned—because of me. I treasured this above God, and trusted it more than God to make me feel valued. I even demanded that others join my delusion. I wanted them to admire my work with awe. I wanted them to worship me.

Not only had I done wrong, but I had to admit that those sins weren't unusual for me. The frustrating week had just caused them to boil over. My selfishness was so strong that even my good desires were twisted back to become mostly about me. I *did* want the good news to impact kids, but sin warped my good intentions until my main reason for doing ministry became how it made me feel. I was right about the helpers—they *were* a problem—but sin jerked at my heart until my main reason for confronting them was to protect my own reputation.

Going Back to the Good News

For the first time that week I really prayed. I confessed my sin. And then I turned to an old favorite, the book of Galatians. I needed to see Jesus, "who gave himself for our sins to deliver us from the present evil age" (Galatians 1:4).

Starting with that opening statement, I read the whole book. I read how God, who knows everything—even the gunk that had been in my heart that week—still set me apart by his grace and showed me his Son. I read how Jesus loved me and gave himself for me. I read how I was cursed, and how Jesus redeemed me by becoming a curse in my place. I read how I'm adopted as God's son—and how, as a son, I'm an heir. My Father shares everything with me, his loved one.

The honors I'd chased after that week were lame in comparison. I felt Paul's words convict me: "But now that you have come to know God, or rather to be known by God, how can you turn back again to the weak and worthless elementary principles of the world?" (Galatians 4:9) I let that soak in. I can be hard as stone—the good news doesn't always crack through to my heart quickly—but I remembered again who I am in Christ. I am a son of God. I wanted to start acting like one.

That meant dying, of course. Dying daily to the world's cheap honors is part of the good news too. It's also the large print in Galatians, literally. Paul ends with a section where he personally handwrites the important takeaway from all the good news that came before: "But far be it from me to boast except in the cross of our Lord Jesus Christ, by which the world has been crucified to me, and I to the world" (Galatians 6:14). A son of God no longer lives for what people think. Instead, his entire reputation is tied to Jesus.

As the terminology suggests, dying can be painful, but it was sweet grace to step out of that self-absorbed muck I'd been stuck in all week. At some point I rediscovered the sense of favor that a son has, and with it came a willingness to let my Father correct me—to let him bend me and shape me.

I set down my Bible and stepped out of my cabin. I started walking toward our meeting area. Right there, sitting alone on a bench, was the teen helper I'd chewed out the day before. It was time to die.

THE CHANGE IN ME

I sat down next to that young man. "Hey, I want to apologize for the way I talked to you yesterday," I told him. "It was mean and I was angry, and I shouldn't have done that."

"No," he said. "I deserved it. You were right. I wasn't doing what I was supposed to."

"It doesn't matter," I said. "I was still wrong. I said those things to make myself feel better instead of to be helpful to you. I'm sorry."

"Okay," he said. "Thanks."

Oh, it would have been *so* easy to stop there. I was powerfully tempted. I could have walked away right then and looked like a big man for having apologized. It could have been an "apology" that actually boosted my reputation—an apology without death. I hesitated. Did I believe my sonship?

I went on. "I've been a jerk," I told him. "I've wanted people to be impressed with me and it wasn't happening and that made me angry, and I took it out on you for no good reason. I know that doesn't make much sense. But you got scolded because I have an ego problem. Will you forgive me?"

He said he would, and I had said what I needed to say. No use pretending I was Super Teacher anymore. The good news had reminded me I wasn't the sensational guy I wanted everyone to think I was. I was a saved guy.

I wish I could tell you everything changed after that and the kids responded well to those final lessons, but I honestly don't remember. It couldn't have gotten *worse*, though. Even if the lessons still didn't seem to get through, there was a change in me that mattered more. My crankiness left. My joy came back. I was teaching for Jesus instead of for what I could get out of it. I knew there might still be irritations, but I was ready to respond by thinking first of others. Those would be chances to practice the kind of love that dies, in little ways, to self.

I also wish I could say it lasted, but it didn't. It doesn't work that way. We never lose the need to stay connected to Jesus. By the time I got home from camp, I was discouraged and angry about the week again, and I needed to reconnect with the good news. I always do, over and over. My soul is incredibly thirsty for recognition and approval and honor. I need to chug Jesus's living water by the bucketful, lest I try to quench that thirst with some other swill.

THE GOOD NEWS FOR TEACHERS

Whether we teach in a ministry setting or lead little ones at home, it's easy to build our self-worth on how well our work with kids seems to be going. In me that tends to show up as arrogance, but it can also result in down-on-yourself discouragement. Pride and self-pity are flip sides of the same thing: being fixated on our performance.

We must be careful. I've spent this whole book essentially urging us to do more for Jesus. In response, we could easily just start trying harder. First we'll feel the pressure. Then if we're successful, we'll end up smug—or if we're unsuccessful, we'll feel discouraged or guilty.

Teachers and parents are particularly susceptible to this. While others in the church might attend Bible studies that focus on the joys of Jesus, most training sessions and lesson plans for *us* are about how to do the job better. Because of this, we of all people especially need to feed on the good news. Vowing to do better next week will do us no good unless we first learn to thank God that he even uses and loves failures like us.

So then, here's *your* good news: when you feel your ministry or parenting twisting inward to be all about you, look outward to Jesus. Repent. Savor the approval *he* gives you. Trust him to fill you again with his Spirit and to revive both your life and your work with kids. He is more sure and lasting and faithful than anything or anyone else you know. *Especially* when you fail, run to Jesus.

I fail all the time. I've written about some successful lessons and good interactions with kids because I want to share helpful examples, but please don't think these happen to me every day. I have lots of frustrating days—many of them clearly my fault and some of them without any apparent cause at all. On such days there's good news all of us must believe.

Believe that God still intends to bless your work with kids.

You won't get it perfectly right, but he always does. Even on the good days, remember to trust only his grace. Give up the idea that it's your gifts and skills that bring kids to God. That's *his* work—and he will use you, flawed as you are. It's majestic, holy work. Keep joining in it. Sound out the good news, and trust the Savior you proclaim to use it to draw souls to himself.

Believe that God still loves you.

Of course your failures as a teacher are massive—the cross is bigger still. Yes, your sin is ever corrupting your message—Jesus forgives, restores, and uses sinful people. He keeps no record of how many times you've had to confess and repent of the same old sin, so keep turning to him. Be a thankful, faith-filled teacher. You're not just telling kids about Jesus—you're resting in him *with* them.

Believe that you're a son or daughter of the Father.

It doesn't matter how poorly you obeyed God today, how sloppily you prepared this week's lesson, or how unloving you felt toward your kids yesterday. Your status cannot change. You're a child of God. You stand alongside your brother Jesus before the throne of heaven. You share his name. You share his access. You share his Spirit. You share the pleasure he feels from the Father. And one day you will share his glory. Get your mind around *that*. Then go out and teach, filled with gratitude and awe.

Believe that it's okay to be weak.

Yes, you are struggling and sinful. Embrace your weakness. Turn to your strong Savior, who in the weakness of the cross triumphed over sin and death and the devil. He will use weakness in your life too. He will make you humble until you rest in *his* strength. Then, like Paul, you'll boast in your weakness instead of trying to hide it. You'll know nothing but the cross, and you'll teach it with power.

All of this is part of showing kids Jesus. It's how you, personally, fit into the good news story.

I'm not adding any list of practical steps you can take to improve your teaching or parenting to the end of this chapter. That's because I want you to focus on the one most practical step of all—deeper faith. *You* must see Jesus. You will do more for him as you know, with growing certainty each day, that he has done more for you.

God gives a stinging rebuke through the prophet Jeremiah: "My people have committed two evils: they have forsaken me, the fountain of living waters, and hewed out cisterns for themselves, broken cisterns that can hold no water" (Jeremiah 2:13). That was me during that week at camp. I turned my back on what God gives me and built my own cisterns to collect worldly honor. I'm tempted this way all the time. I amass Bible knowledge, ministry skills, approval from pastors, and praise from other parents—and I drink them in. They fill churchy cisterns that have an appearance of godliness, but they're swamp water nonetheless.

Most teachers and parents I know struggle to have a living, resting, joyful partnership with God in their work with kids. Like me, they get sidetracked by insecurity or self-glory. They fear failure, or they worship the approval of others and end up hard-hearted.

What a difference a tender heart makes. A heart soaked in the softening oil of the good news will lose its stiffness and bend to the will of God. It will come to find sin distasteful. It will thrill to sing of Jesus. It will grow a robust, joyful holiness that attracts both young and old to the Savior.

Conclusion
The True Minister

The last word in this book belongs to Charles Spurgeon, who spoke with more flourish than I can muster and more sharpness than I dare. When I read Spurgeon's sermons, I try to imagine him as he preached in nineteenth-century London. On April 14, 1867, he stepped to the podium at the Royal Agricultural Hall to speak on "The Unsearchable Riches of Christ."

At the time, Spurgeon was the world's most popular preacher, and the Agricultural Hall one of the world's grandest buildings. It had a seventy-five-foot-high, arched glass ceiling and seating for ten thousand people. Twice that many arrived that Sunday morning. They packed in to hear Spurgeon—without the aid of modern microphones—boom out his message based on the words of Paul: "To me, though I am the very least of all the saints, this grace was given, to preach to the Gentiles the unsearchable riches of Christ" (Ephesians 3:8).

Spurgeon's voice traveled farther than he could have imagined. One day not long ago, I downloaded a reading of this sermon and discovered a gem. Spurgeon said what I've been trying to say all through this book. Here's a condensed excerpt from that sermon:

Although our Apostle [Paul] . . . knew and confessed his weakness, there is one thing which never troubled him—he was never perplexed as to the subject of his ministry. . . . From his first sermon to his last, when he laid down his neck upon the block to seal his testimony with his blood, Paul preached Christ and nothing but Christ. . . .

The true minister is he who can preach Christ. . . . If Christ crucified is the great delight of his soul, the very marrow of his teaching, the fatness of his ministry, he has proved his calling as an ambassador of Christ. . . .

Oh, to speak of Christ alone!—to be tied and bound to this one theme forever; to speak only of Jesus and of the amazing Love of the glorious Son of God, who, "though He was rich, yet for our sakes became poor." This is the Subject which is both "seed for the sower and bread for the eater." This is the live Coal for the lips of the preacher, and the master Key to the heart of the hearer! This is the Tune for the minstrels of earth, and the Song for the harpers of Heaven! Lord, teach it to us more and more, and we will tell it out to others! [1]

Since first discovering this sermon, I've learned that there was a young Sunday school teacher from America in Spurgeon's audience that day—by the name of Dwight L. Moody. He returned from London captivated, determined to speak of Christ more than ever, and ended up building the largest gospel-preaching ministry of his generation.

That's how it goes. One teacher inspires another, and that one tells a student. One parent encourages another, and that one tells his kids. The students and kids grow up and tell still others—and each generation of believers rediscovers the beauty of Jesus.

How will you be part of that? The next time you enter your classroom or meet with the youth group or sit down with your kid at the kitchen table, what will you do to be a true minister? How will you, like so many faithful teachers before you, show them Jesus?

Twelve Answers to the Objection That Teaching God's Free Grace Leads to Lax Obedience

One of the main objections I hear when I talk about good-news teaching is that it sounds soft on sin and the need to obey God. When I say that teaching absolutely free grace in Jesus leads us to obey him out of gratitude, from the heart, people sometimes think it sounds like I'm saying we don't have to obey unless we feel like it.

That's not true at all! We must daily say no to sin even if that sin feels good at the moment—and sometimes it does. Explanations of how good-news teaching *helps* obedience rather than working against it are sprinkled throughout this book. However, since many people struggle with this question, I thought I'd also collect those explanations and put them in one place.

1. Unless our hearts are in it, we haven't fully obeyed God in the first place. If we're happy merely to manage a reluctant sort of good behavior, we're aiming too low. God commands us to obey from the heart (Deuteronomy 30:2). He says repentance must come from the heart (1 Kings 8:48). He tells us to forgive from the heart (Matthew 18:35). And Jesus said the great and first commandment is, "Love the Lord your God with all your heart" (Matthew 22:37). When teaching helps kids to obey gladly, out of heartfelt gratitude rather than under compulsion, it isn't being soft about God's law but rather very serious about it. It's setting the bar high—where God sets it.

2. *Obedience that's grounded in love overcomes how we feel at the moment.* It's a mistake to think that love-based obedience is captive to feelings. Consider the people you love. Even if you love them dearly, sometimes you don't *feel* like serving them—but since you love them you'll serve them anyway. Love harbors a desire that goes beyond how you feel at the moment. Believers who love God have a lasting, underlying desire to obey him, even amid temptation and mixed feelings. That's the nature of love.

3. *The suspicion that saved people use grace as an excuse to sin has too small a view of salvation and grace.* If the only thing God did for us was to forgive us—then okay, maybe grace would make us think we could sin as much as we like. But in Romans 6, Paul explains that even though we enjoy God's grace, we don't go on sinning because that grace includes much more than forgiveness. We're joined to Christ. We're alive in him and growing spiritually. Due to this, we have a new model for obedience that's rooted in the Spirit's work in us. When kids learn a view of salvation that includes delight in the grace of "a holy calling" (2 Timothy 1:9), there's no worry that teaching such grace might lead them to think sin is okay.

4. *Knowing we're surely saved can't lead to lax behavior if we understand how grand our future happiness will be.* Another thing we know if our view of salvation is big, like it should be, is that we'll be overjoyed one day to be completely free of sin. The better we understand the beauty of this—and are *sure* it's coming because God is gracious—the more we'll want to overcome sin in *this* life. Kids gripped by grace have a taste of heaven. It makes them hungry to live like heaven-bound people now.

5. The idea that God's grace might let us get away with sin is not how reborn people should think. Paul also says in Romans 6 that our new life has a new attitude. The old attitude that asked, "How much can I get away with?" belongs to our old, worldly lives. We're set free of that. It should no longer occur to us to obey just enough to avoid punishment. If your teaching panders to that kind of thinking by avoiding grace, you're using the old, worldly motives instead of alive-in-Christ ones. Christians obey because they're sold out to Jesus. The law-based mentality does the minimum to get by; a love-based mentality does the most it can. Which is a fuller obedience?

6. It's not possible for us to do godly things consistently unless our hearts are captivated by God. We might bring ourselves to resist a sin here and there when it's easy, when we're feeling extra-determined, or when others are watching. Most of the rest of the time, however, our hearts win out—we serve what (or whom) we love. The only way to become a more consistently obedient person is to push out sinful loves by replacing them with a bigger love for God.

7. We can't really obey God if we're unsure of his pleasure toward us. If we aren't convinced he actually loves us, forever and unfailingly, everything we do for him will only be a scheme to impress him and try to earn or keep his love. That's manipulation, not obedience. We'll actually be doing our acts of "obedience" for ourselves—and to save ourselves. Such selfishness and misplaced faith isn't godly behavior.

8. Knowing God's grace lets us get serious about God's law without falling into despair. A teacher who fails to teach God's grace has to be careful not to push kids too hard to obey, because they can easily get either discouraged or proud. It's easier when kids are sure of God's grace no matter what. Then a teacher can be much *more forceful* in urging them to obey. There's less worry that even very hard teaching about obedience will lead to despair or self-righteousness. More grace allows harder teaching about sin, not softer teaching.

9. To become more effective at fighting sin and at obeying, we must focus on believing the good news. The most fundamental of all the good works God requires is belief: "This is the work of God, that you believe in him whom he has sent" (John 6:29). Unbelief is at the root of all other sin. Unless kids learn to strengthen their belief in Jesus by hearing and responding to the good news, their fight against sin will have a lousy strategy. They'll struggle with surface sins while ignoring the heart—and get nowhere. The good-news strategy is far more serious about whole-life obedience than an approach that just takes pot shots at certain visible sins.

*10. Unless our good works spring from belief in Jesus, they aren't even actually **good**.* Faith is so central that "whatever does not proceed from faith is sin" (Romans 14:23). Elsewhere, the Bible says, "without faith it is impossible to please him, for whoever would draw near to God must believe that he exists and that he rewards those who seek him" (Hebrews 11:6). When kids learn about and believe the gracious rewards that are ours in Jesus, they've laid the mandatory foundation for *true* obedience.

11. God means for his kindness to motivate us to obey. Sure, there always are some people who presume that God's forgiveness comes easily and take their sin lightly as a result. However, when Paul addresses this problem, he doesn't say that the solution is to stop teaching grace. Instead, he explains that grace is designed to have the opposite effect: "Do you presume on the riches of his kindness and forbearance and patience, not knowing that God's kindness is meant to lead you to repentance?" (Romans 2:4). God's kindness, when properly understood, leads to repentance. Kids see how richly his love has reached down to them—with the compassion of the cross—and are compelled to hate sin like he does.

12. Our experience agrees with what the Bible teaches: people who love God's grace also love to obey him. I have never, ever met a kid who was powerfully gripped by grace and, as a result of appreciating so fully how God loves him in spite of his sin, went around doing all kinds of sin just because he knew he could get away with it. That doesn't happen. A true appreciation for grace always brings humility, which makes kids *willing* to be obedient. We ought to expect this based on passages about grace such as Titus 2:11–12: "For the grace of

God has appeared, bringing salvation for all people, training us to re-nounce ungodliness and worldly passions, and to live self-controlled, upright, and godly lives in the present age." The kids I know who truly have joy in Christ fit that passage. They obey happily, even when they think no one's looking. It's the kids who feel pressure who end up liv-ing a double life—who put on a godly image at home or church but sneak around sinning at other times.

****

Maybe you've read all this, and you still hesitate. Maybe teaching that much grace still just feels wrong.

Well, *of course* it does. The good news is ridiculous by the world's sensibilities. It violates all we know about how to force sin-trapped people to comply.

But we are no longer trapped; we're free in Christ. We who have felt the power of the good news know that we're most eager to obey when we're most delighted with Jesus. Although we still struggle with sin, we're destined to worship eternally with the best of moti-vations, and by God's grace our lives today already display some of that wonder.

Endnotes

Chapter 1: The One-Note Teacher

1. Charles H. Spurgeon, "Christ, the Glory of His People," in *Metropolitan Tabernacle Pulpit: Sermons Preached and Revised by C. H. Spurgeon During the year 1868* (Pasadena, TX: Pilgrim, 1970), 14:467.

2. John Owen, "Christologia, or A Declaration of the Glorious Mystery of the Person of Christ," in *The Works of John Owen* (London: Richard Baynes, 1826), 12:184.

Chapter 2: The God Report Card

1. Owen, "A Practical Exposition on the CXXXth Psalm," in *The Works of John Owen*, 14:22.

2. The term "therapeutic" comes from the 2003–2005 National Study of Youth and Religion, described by Kenda Creasy Dean, *Almost Christian: What the Faith of Our Teenagers Is Telling the American Church* (New York: Oxford University Press, 2010).

Chapter 3: The "Gospel Day" Trap

1. Richard Sibbes, "Bowels Opened, or Expository Sermons on Canticles IV:16, V, VI," in *The Complete Works of Richard Sibbes* (Edinburgh: James Nichol, 1862), 2:142.

2. This phenomenon has been confirmed by many studies, some claiming the rate to be as high as 90 percent. I trust the more conservative figure of 59 percent, based on research by the Barna Group and reported by David Kinnaman, *You Lost Me: Why Young Christians Are Leaving Church and Rethinking Faith* (Grand Rapids, MI: Baker, 2011), 23.

3. Walter Marshall, *The Gospel Mystery of Sanctification: Growing in Holiness by Living in Union with Christ*, trans. Bruce H. McRae (Eugene, OR: Wipf & Stock, 2005), 112.

4. Serge, *Sonship*, 3rd ed. (Greensboro, NC: New Growth Press, 2013), 153. This diagram can also be found in *The Gospel-Centered Life* by Robert H. Thune and Will Walker (Greensboro, NC: New Growth, 2011), 13.

5. Serge, *Gospel Identity: Discovering Who You Really Are*, (Greensboro, NC: New Growth, 2012); Serge, *Gospel Growth: Becoming a Faith-Filled Person* (Greensboro, NC: New Growth, 2012); Serge, *Gospel Love: Grace, Relationships, and Everything that Gets in the Way* (Greensboro, NC: New Growth, 2012).

Chapter 4: The Factory-Preset Fourth Grader

1. Horatius Bonar, *The Everlasting Righteousness* (London: James Nisbet, 1873), 188.

2. Janet Elise Rosenbaum, "Patient Teenagers? A Comparison of the Sexual Behavior of Virginity Pledgers and Matched Nonpledgers," *Pediatrics*, 123, no. 1 (2009): e110–e120.

3. This application of 1 John 2:15, and the inspiration for the king-of-the-hill illustration, come from Thomas Chalmers, *The Expulsive Power of a New Affection* (Edinburgh: Thomas Constable, 1855).

Chapter 5: The Mom in Queen Esther's Bedroom

1. John Calvin, *Commentaries on the Epistles of Paul the Apostle to the Philippians, Colossians and Thessalonians*, trans. John Pringle (Grand Rapids, MI: Baker, 2003), 145.

2. G. K. Beale and D. A. Carson, eds., *Commentary on the New Testament Use of the Old Testament* (Grand Rapids, MI: Baker Academic, 2007).

Chapter 6: The Talking Donkey and Jesus

1. Matthew Henry, *Commentary on the Whole Bible* (McLean, VA: MacDonald Publishing), 5:935.

2. My list of ways to teach Christ from the Old Testament corresponds roughly to those proposed by Sidney Greidanus in his books, *Preaching Christ from the Old Testament: A Contemporary Hermeneutical Method* (Grand Rapids, MI: Eerdmans, 1999), 203–225; and *Preaching Christ from Genesis: Foundations for Expository Sermons* (Grand Rapids, MI: Eerdmans, 2007), 2–6.

Chapter 7: The Longest List in Church

1. Ralph Erskine, "Gospel Sonnets," in *The Poetical Works of Ralph Erskine* (Aberdeen: George and Robert King, 1858), 95.

2. "Heidelberg Catechism," *Psalter Hymnal,* Q & A 52 (Grand Rapids, MI: Board of Publications of the Christian Reformed Church, 1976), 26.

Chapter 8: The Grapes that Taught Good News

1. John Arrowsmith, *Armilla Catechetica: A Chain of Principles* (Edinburgh: Thomas Turnbull, 1822), 208.

Chapter 9: The War on Sin and Bad Songs

1. Thomas Watson, *The Doctrine of Repentance* (Edinburgh: Banner of Truth, 2009), 102.

2. This question is adapted from other Serge materials: see *Sonship,* 3rd ed. (Greensboro, NC: New Growth, 2013), 46; and *The Gospel-Centered Life, Leader's Guide* (Greensboro, NC: New Growth, 2011), 26.

3. The value of repeated repentance is described well by Serge in its book, *Gospel Identity: Discovering Who You Really Are* (Greensboro, NC: New Growth, 2012), 114.

4. The shark illustration comes from Serge staffers Stu Batstone and Deborah Harrell. Deborah and I first put the illustration into chart form when developing sample lessons for a discipleship course for children.

Chapter 10: The Class in the Boiler Room

1. Thomas Manton, "A Practical Exposition of the Lord's Prayer," *The Complete Works of Thomas Manton* (London: James Nisbet, 1870), 1:64.

2. John Calvin, *Institutes of the Christian Religion*, trans. Ford Lewis Battles (Philadelphia: Westminster, 1960), 2:850.

3. Calvin, *Institutes,* 2:852.

Chapter 11: The Skis I Never Wore

1. John Newton, *The Works of the Rev. John Newton* (Edinburgh: Thomas Nelson and Peter Brown, 1836), 211.

Conclusion: The True Minister

1. Charles H. Spurgeon, "The Unsearchable Riches of Christ," last modified April 29, 2013, http://www.spurgeongems.org/vols13-15/chs745.pdf.

Index of Bible Lessons

mission
propelled by good news

At Serge we believe that mission begins through the gospel of Jesus Christ bringing God's grace into the lives of believers. This good news also sustains and empowers us to cross nations and cultures to bring the gospel of grace to those whom God is calling to himself.

As a cross-denominational, reformed sending agency with more than two hundred missionaries and twenty-five teams in five continents, we are always looking for people who are ready to take the next step in sharing Christ through:

- **Short-term Teams:** One- to two-week trips oriented around serving overseas ministries while equipping the local church for mission

- **Internships:** Eight-week to nine-month opportunities to learn about missions through serving with our overseas ministry teams

- **Apprenticeships:** Intensive twelve- to twenty-four-month training and ministry opportunities for those discerning their call to cross-cultural ministry

- **Career:** One- to five-year appointments designed to nurture you for a lifetime of ministry

 Grace at the Fray

Visit us online at: serge.org/mission

newgrowthpress.com

spiritual renewal
resources for you

Disciples who are motivated and empowered by grace to reach out to a broken world are handmade, not mass-produced. Serge intentionally grows disciples through curricula, discipleship experiences, and training programs.

Resources for Every Stage of Growth

Serge offers grace-based, gospel-centered studies for every stage of the Christian journey. Every level of our materials focuses on essential aspects of how the Spirit transforms and motivates us through the gospel of Jesus Christ.

- **101**: The Gospel-Centered Series
  Gospel-centered studies on Christian growth, community, work, parenting, and more

- **201**: The Gospel Transformation Series
  These studies go a step deeper into gospel transformation, involve homework and more in-depth Bible study

- **301**: The Sonship Course and Serge Individual Mentoring

Mentored Sonship

For more than twenty-five years Serge has been discipling ministry leaders around the world through our Sonship course to help them experience the freedom and joy of having the gospel transform every part of their lives. A personal discipler will help you apply what you are learning to the daily struggles and situations you face, as well as, model what a gospel-centered faith looks and feels like.

Discipler Training Course

Serge's Discipler Training Course helps you gain biblical understanding and practical wisdom you need to disciple others so they experience substantive, lasting growth in their lives. Available for on-site training or via distance learning, our training programs are ideal for ministry leaders, small group leaders or those seeking to grow in their ability to disciple effectively.

 Grace at the Fray   **Find more resources at serge.org**

newgrowthpress.com